Retirement Portfolios Workbook

T0327661

Founded in 1807, John Wiley & Sons is the oldest independent publishing company in the United States. With offices in North America, Europe, Australia, and Asia, Wiley is globally committed to developing and marketing print and electronic products and services for our customers' professional and personal knowledge and understanding.

The Wiley Finance series contains books written specifically for finance and investment professionals as well as sophisticated individual investors and their financial advisors. Book topics range from portfolio management to e-commerce, risk management, financial engineering, valuation and financial instrument analysis, as well as much more.

For a list of available titles, please visit our Web site at www. WileyFinance.com.

Retirement Portfolios Workbook

Theory, Construction, and Management

MICHAEL J. ZWECHER

WILEY

John Wiley & Sons, Inc.

For general information on our other products and services or for technical support,
please contact our Customer Care Department within the United States at (800)
762-2974, outside the United States at (317) 572-3993 or fax (317) 572-4002.

Wiley also publishes its books in a variety of electronic formats. Some content that
appears in print may not be available in electronic books. For more information about
Wiley products, visit our web site at www.wiley.com.

ISBN 978-0-470-55987-1

10 9 8 7 6 5 4 3 2 1

Contents

Preface

This workbook is the companion to *Retirement Portfolios: Theory, Construction, and Management*. The workbook allows you to delve deeper into the main book's topics and create the proficiency required for professional designation as a life-cycle investment or retirement investment professional.

The problems in Part One of this workbook are correlated with each chapter. By reading each chapter and performing corresponding chapter problems, you will better understand the problems and assimilate the material in the text. The readings and problems provide mutual reinforcement.

With the exception of a handful of warm-ups, the workbook problems are each designed to make a point directly related to the text, the larger discussion of retirement income in particular, and portfolios in general. In designing these problems, it is assumed that you are well versed in financial products and portfolio management; broadly familiar with portfolio theory; and competent but "rusty" in mathematics. The problems are designed to take you through the conceptual and bring you to the practical—that is, the problems should build you up rather than trip you up.

In Part Two of this workbook, detailed solutions are provided for every problem. In some cases, the problems require tools that are more advanced than expected from the typical user. In such cases, I try to provide enough detail to help walk you through the problem and get to the issue that the problem is trying to address.

Some of the problems address concepts, but many are trying to walk you through what you may want to do in practice, or how you can build tools that you can readily use. If you come away from a problem saying to yourself either "I get it, that's good to know" or "Well that would be easy to add to my practice," then I will have accomplished my goal. I want you to come away from these problems knowing how to build a viable business that you can be proud of.

Most of the questions are associated with Chapters 1 through 9 and Chapter 15. These 10 chapters constitute the bulk of the material that is suitable to a workbook format. For the other chapters, I have created thought provoking questions and provided some ancillary material that you will find useful in practice.

Just as the main book went to great lengths to avoid promoting any particular firm's products or techniques, the same is true of the tools used here. I do not mean to endorse or promote any particular tool or software for working through these problems.

BEFORE YOU GET STARTED: TOOLS YOU'LL NEED TO COMPLETE THE EXERCISES

Most books on investments focus on single-period investment problems and topics. However, the focus here is on the long term, where issues like cumulative returns and cumulative risk take on added importance. In a sense, you can think of the emphasis of both books as adding through time instead of adding across assets or choosing a particular asset at a particular point in time.

Most of the problems in this workbook can be easily handled by tools that you use every day. Occasionally, we'll use the tools that you are used to using in an unfamiliar way, or we have to tweak the tools to make them more amenable to multiperiod analysis.

In the next few pages we'll first cover a boot-camp version of some formulas related to present and future values of annuities, both level and growing. I hope that this first part is familiar territory for you.

Next, we switch gears to cover the basics of asset returns useful for multiperiod problems. We cover the random nature of returns and the ways that it is typically shown. We then adapt the typical view to cover the multiperiod problem of building a portfolio through time. This second part may be somewhat new, but it is only a small change from what you are used to—and to make this topic more interesting, we cover a common but dangerous fallacy.

We also cover a brief description of efficient frontiers and the capital-market line. These are concepts that are fundamental building blocks of modern portfolio construction. While conceptually appealing, there are extraordinary difficulties with trying to build portfolios that are mean/variance efficient. That few clients seem interested in buying mean/variance efficient portfolios is covered in Chapter 2; even economically optimizing, rational investors may prefer portfolios that protect lifestyle rather than meet the overly simple criteria of mean/variance optimization. Those caveats in place, the concept of the capital market line is still extraordinarily useful.

Annuity Formulas

All of these formulas are related to finding present values or future values of cash flows. Annuities are payments that are expected to recur at a stated frequency. Annuities in our usage can either be level payments or payments that grow at a constant rate. Annuities may be of fixed duration or potentially infinite duration. Throughout most of the workbook, I'll differentiate between the typical financial textbook definition of annuities used here and the colloquial usage of the term as a way to refer to the insurance-related subset of annuities.

I'll go through the derivation of the formulas, but your main interest will probably be in the formulas themselves. The formulas are easy to incorporate into spreadsheets for a wide variety of uses. I go through the derivation to try to pitch the idea so that you don't need to memorize the formulas, you just have to remember the simple idea behind them.

Although the formulas for annuities were more useful before the advent of spreadsheet programs, it is still helpful to take a brief detour and provide some background material on payment streams, present values, and future values that you might find helpful. Also, by reading through this part, it should help brush away some cobwebs and make the remainder of the workbook more enjoyable.

The General Rule Underlying Annuities Some formulas have 1,001 uses. The annuity formula is one of them. So let me present it in a slightly different way that starts out looking like rather unappealing math but allows you to adapt the formula for a multitude of uses and doesn't require that you commit much to memory.

First, let's look at *geometric sums,* defining the sum of a geometric series as S_N:

$$S_N = x + x^2 + x^3 + \cdots + x^N$$

This series is hard to add up by itself and would have to be added term by term if we couldn't find a way to simplify the problem, but we have a trick: Multiply every element of the sum by x, that is,

$$xS_N = x^2 + x^3 + x^4 + \cdots + x^{N+1}$$

If we subtract the second expression from the first, we calculate the difference $S_N - xS_N$, and all that we are left with is the following:

$$S_N - xS_N = x - x^{N+1}$$

Our trick allowed us to create what is called a telescoping series. This is all you ever have to commit to memory and from which all of the annuity results follow. The previous expression can be simplified to

$$S_N = \left(\frac{x - x^{N+1}}{1 - x} \right)$$

Ordinary Annuities   For present value of an ordinary annuity, replace x with $\left(\frac{1}{1+r}\right)$, where r is the discount rate and N is the number of years in the annuity. Making the substitution and performing some messy algebra yields the following familiar formula:

$$S_N = \left(\frac{x - x^{N+1}}{1 - x} \right) = \frac{\dfrac{1}{1+r} - \left(\dfrac{1}{1+r}\right)^{N+1}}{1 - \dfrac{1}{1+r}} = \left(\frac{1}{1+r}\right)\left(\frac{1}{1+r}\right)\left(\frac{1 - \left(\dfrac{1}{1+r}\right)^N}{r} \right)$$

$$= \frac{1}{r}\left(1 - \left(\frac{1}{1+r}\right)^N\right) = PV_{Annuity}(N, r)$$

The typical uses for this formula are in permutations of the following:

$$Value = Pmt \times PV_{Annuity}(N, r),$$

Generally the preceding is used either for figuring out the present value of a payments stream given N, r, Pmt or in figuring out the payment stream required to pay off a present value given N, r, $Value$.

The formulas that we will go through are very easy and useful to set up in a spreadsheet. For your spreadsheets, try the following example:

Data	
R	0.04
N	10.00
Intermediate Step	
1 + r	1.04
Calculations	
1/r	25
$1/(1 + r)^N$	0.675564
$1 - 1/(1 + r)^N$	0.324436
Result (rounded)	8.11

Example: A \$12,000 annual payment annuity for 10 years at 4 percent would have an unrounded present value of \$97,330.75.

Annuities Growing at a Constant Rate   If the payment is growing at a constant rate g, then instead of using the substitution $x = \dfrac{1}{1+r}$, use $x = \dfrac{1+g}{1+r}$. In this case the formula changes a little bit.

$$S_N = \left(\frac{x - x^{N+1}}{1-x}\right) = \frac{\dfrac{1+g}{1+r} - \left(\dfrac{1+g}{1+r}\right)^{N+1}}{1 - \dfrac{1+g}{1+r}} = \left(\frac{\dfrac{1+g}{1+r}}{\dfrac{1}{1+r}}\right)\left(\frac{1 - \left(\dfrac{1+g}{1+r}\right)^{N}}{r-g}\right)$$

$$= \frac{1+g}{r-g}\left(1 - \left(\frac{1+g}{1+r}\right)^{N}\right) = PV_{Annuity}^{Growing}(N, r, g)$$

If $g < r$ and N becomes large, then the term on the right, inside of the parentheses, approaches zero and the formula will approach $\dfrac{1+g}{r-g}$, which may look familiar to many of you as the "guts" of the dividend growth formula for fundamental valuation of equity $p = \dfrac{D_0(1+g)}{r-g}$, where D_0 is the current dividend.

For your spreadsheets, try the following example:

Data	
R	0.05
G	0.02
N	10.00
Intermediate Steps	
$1 + r$	1.05
$1 + g$	1.02
Calculations	
$(1 + g)/(r - g)$	34
$A = (1 + g)/(1 + r)$	0.971427
A^N	0.748357
$1 - 1/(1 + r)^N$	0.251643
Result	8.56

Example: A \$12,000 annual payment annuity for 10 years at 5 percent, growing at 2 percent would have an unrounded present value of \$102,670.40.

Deferred Annuities For annuities that are deferred, you have two choices, either subtract from individual elements representing the deferral or use the previous formula to subtract from an annuity of the same duration as the deferral.

Alternative Compounding Periods If the compounding period is something other than annual, say M times per year, then in all of the formulas replace the annual rate r with r/M and replace N with $M*N$ years. One thing to remember is that the payments of the annuity need to match up with the frequency. For example, if the annuity pays \$12,000 and the compounding and payments are monthly then the monthly payments of \$1,000 should be used.

$$
S_N = \left(\frac{x - x^{N+1}}{1 - x} \right) \rightarrow \frac{\dfrac{1}{1 + \dfrac{r}{M}} - \left(\dfrac{1}{1 + \dfrac{r}{M}} \right)^{NM+1}}{1 - \dfrac{1}{1 + \dfrac{r}{M}}} = \frac{\left(\dfrac{1}{1 + \dfrac{r}{M}} \right) \left(1 - \left(\dfrac{1}{1 + \dfrac{r}{M}} \right)^{NM} \right)}{\left(\dfrac{1}{1 + \dfrac{r}{M}} \right) \dfrac{r}{M}}
$$

$$
= \frac{M}{r} \left(1 - \left(\frac{1}{1 + \dfrac{r}{M}} \right)^{NM} \right) = PV_{Annuity}\left(NM, \frac{r}{M} \right)
$$

For your spreadsheets, try the following example:

Data	
R	0.04
N	10.00
M	4
Intermediate Step	
1 + r/M	1.01
Calculations	
A = 1/(1 + r/M)	0.99099
A^{NM}	0.671653
1 − 1/(1 + r)^{NM}	0.328347
Result	32.83

Example: A \$12,000 annual payment annuity for 10 years at 4 percent, payable quarterly would have an unrounded present value of \$98,504.06.

Constant Growth with Alternative Compounding Periods If the compounding period is something other than annual, say M times per year, then in all of the formulas replace the annual rate r with r/M, g with g/M and replace N with $M*N$ years. Once again, remember that the payments of the annuity need to match up with the frequency. For example, if the annuity pays \$12,000 and the compounding and payments are monthly then the monthly payments of \$1,000 should be used.

$$S_N = \left(\frac{x - x^{N+1}}{1-x}\right) \rightarrow \frac{1 + \dfrac{g}{M} - \dfrac{1 + \dfrac{g}{M}}{1 + \dfrac{r}{M}}\left(\dfrac{1 + \dfrac{g}{M}}{1 + \dfrac{r}{M}}\right)^{NM+1}}{1 - \dfrac{1 + \dfrac{g}{M}}{1 + \dfrac{r}{M}}} = \left(\dfrac{1 + \dfrac{g}{M}}{1 + \dfrac{r}{M}}\right)\left(\dfrac{1 - \left(\dfrac{1 + \dfrac{g}{M}}{1 + \dfrac{r}{M}}\right)^{NM}}{\dfrac{\left(1 + \dfrac{r}{M}\right) - \left(1 + \dfrac{g}{M}\right)}{1 + \dfrac{r}{M}}}\right)$$

$$= \frac{M\left(1 + \dfrac{g}{M}\right)}{r - g}\left(1 - \left(\dfrac{1 + \dfrac{g}{M}}{1 + \dfrac{r}{M}}\right)^{NM}\right) = PV_{Growing\_Annuity}\left(NM, \frac{r}{M}, \frac{g}{M}\right)$$

For your spreadsheets, try the following example:

Data	
R	0.05
G	0.02
N	10.00
M	4
Intermediate Steps	
$1 + r/M$	1.01
$1 + g/M$	1.005
Calculations	
$A = M(1 + g/M)/(r - g)$	134
$B = (1 + g/M)/(1 + r/M)$	0.992593
B^{NM}	0.742747
$1 - B^{NM}$	0.257253
Result	34.47

Example: A \$12,000 annual payment annuity for 10 years at $r = 5$ percent, $g = 2$ percent, payable quarterly would have an unrounded present value of \$103,415.50.

Time Required Paying off a Debt   One of the reasons that this formula is so useful is that it makes it easy to answer Problems about the length of time required to pay off a loan at different payment levels. Suppose that we owe a total of V and make payments of P *per period*. We include the possibility of a growth rate in required payments although generally $g = 0$. With a little algebra we can see that since

$$V = P \frac{1 + \dfrac{g}{M}}{\dfrac{r}{M} - \dfrac{g}{M}} \left(1 - \left(\frac{1 + \dfrac{g}{M}}{1 + \dfrac{r}{M}} \right)^{NM} \right)$$

$$N = \frac{1}{M} \left(\frac{Ln\left(1 - \dfrac{V}{P}\left(\dfrac{\dfrac{r}{M} - \dfrac{g}{M}}{1 + \dfrac{g}{M}} \right) \right)}{Ln\left(\dfrac{1 + \dfrac{g}{M}}{1 + \dfrac{r}{M}} \right)} \right)$$

If we place the formula into a spreadsheet, it is easy to see how the time to pay off the loan amount owed can be impacted by changing P. The most common use for this formula is in the estimated time to pay off a mortgage if some extra amount is regularly included with the monthly payment.

For your spreadsheets, try the following example:

Data	
V	\$100,000
P	\$2,500
R	0.06
M	12
G	0.03

Intermediate Steps	
r/M	0.0050
g/M	0.0025
1 + g/M	1.005

Intermediate Steps	
$1 + r/M$	1.0025
V/P	40.00

Calculations	
$V/P(r/M - g/M)$	0.10
$V/P(r/M - g/M)/(1 + g/M)$	0.099751
$A = \ln(1 - V/P(r/M - g/M)/(1 + g/M))$	−0.10508
$B = \ln((1 + g/M)/(1 + r/M))$	−0.00249
Result $(1/M)(A/B)$	3.52 years

Try on your own: Notice the intuitive result that if the payments are constant rather than growing, the payment stream will last longer.

One special case that needs to be noted: if $r = g$ then $x = \dfrac{1 + \dfrac{g}{M}}{1 + \dfrac{r}{M}} = 1$

and if you try to simply calculate the formula you end up trying to calculate $\dfrac{Ln(1)}{Ln(1)} = \dfrac{0}{0}$, which is undefined. If you go back to the original definition of the sum S_N, you see that if $r = g$ the sum $S_N = N$, so in this special case the number of payments to pay off an annuity will simply be determined by the value of the loan divided by the size of the payments.

Future Value   For future values of ordinary annuities, the date of reckoning is made on the date that last deposit is made. This means that there is one less compounding period and instead of running from x to x_N, the sum S_N runs from 1 to x_{N-1}

$$S_N^{FV} = \left(\frac{1 - x^N}{1 - x}\right) = \left(\frac{1 - (1+r)^N}{1 - (1+r)}\right) = \frac{1}{r}\left(\frac{(1+r)^N - 1}{1}\right)$$

If the payments are growing, replace the value x with $x = (1 + g)(1 + r)$. The previous expression is altered only slightly to

$$S_N^{FV} = \left(\frac{1 - x^N}{1 - x}\right) = \left(\frac{1 - ((1+r)(1+g))^N}{1 - (1+r)(1+g)}\right)$$
$$= \frac{1}{r + g + rg}\left(\frac{(1+r)^N(1+g)^N - 1}{1}\right)$$

In this case, the substitutions required for compounding at a rate that is not annual is left as an exercise.

For your spreadsheets, try the following example:

Data	
R	0.06
M	12
G	0.02
N	10
Intermediate Steps	
r/M	0.0050
g/M	0.001667
1 + g/M	1.005
1 + r/M	1.001667
Calculations	
$A = r/M + g/M + rg/M^2$	0.006675
$B = 1/A$	149.8127
$C = (1 + r/M)^{NM}(1 + g/M)^{NM}$	2.221846
Result $(C-1)*B$	183.05

Example: \$500 saved monthly for 10 years at r = 6 percent, g = 2 percent, would have an unrounded future value of \$91,524.06.

Notation of Asset Returns and Basics

In single period analysis, we usually define returns on assets by $r_{t,t+1} = \dfrac{P_{t+1} - P_t}{P_t}$, where r is the percentage return on the asset and P represents the price of the asset observed at period t and $t + 1$. The return r is a random variable and is usually written as consisting of a fixed mean (expected return) plus a random component, representing unexpected movement over the period t to $t + 1$, that is, $r_{t,t+1} = \mu + \varepsilon_{t,t+1}$. The random component has a variance that is also generally assumed to be constant so that $\mathrm{var}(\varepsilon_{t,t+1}) = \sigma^2_{t,t+1} = \sigma^2$.

The usual notation is that there are $i = 1, 2, ..., N$ assets. The return on i^{th} asset is usually just written as r_i with the t subscripts subsumed so that the focus can be placed on portfolios combining larger or smaller subsets of the M assets. The temporal nature of the returns gets lost in the translation as the previous equation is usually rewritten $r_i = \mu_i + \varepsilon_i$ and $\mathrm{var}(\varepsilon_i) = \sigma^2_i$. This has the impact of making an assumption that the returns are identically distributed through time. The distribution of returns looks the same for ABC today as it did five years ago.

When we construct portfolios of assets, return is usually denoted r_p. The heavy machinery of the central limit theorem and the normal distribution is usually brought in at this point. For simplicity, we usually start by constructing an equally weighted portfolio such that for a portfolio of N assets $r_p = \frac{1}{N}\sum_{i=1}^{N} r_i$. Importantly, this means that $\mu_p = \frac{1}{N}\sum_{i=1}^{N} \mu_i$ and that $\sigma_p^2 = \frac{1}{N^2}\sum_{i=1}^{N} \sigma_i^2$; if variance is constant across assets then $\sigma_p^2 = \frac{1}{N^2} N\sigma^2 = \frac{\sigma^2}{N}$. That the variance of a sample average is lower than the variance of an individual element of the sample is a property of random variables that is not specific to returns. Since standard deviation is the square root of variance, the standard deviation of a sample average becomes $\sigma_p = \frac{\sigma}{\sqrt{N}}$. Confusing the standard deviation of a sample average with the standard deviation for cumulative returns is the source of one of the most common and dangerous fallacies in finance.

> *The Fallacy:* The long-run risk of a portfolio being lower than the risk in the short run.

This fallacy shows up far too often, usually backed up by the arithmetic for sample averages to claim that the volatility of a portfolio declines over time at the square root of T. A typical example is that if the annual volatility is 30 percent, then the volatility over 16 years would only be 7.5 percent. Not only is this a fallacy, but it also leads to results that are somewhat humorous. An implication is that if we run the problem in reverse, the shorter the interval, the higher the volatility. If the annual volatility were 30 percent, then the implication of the fallacy would be that the volatility over one trading day would be about 480 percent.

The fallacy, mistaking properties of an average of random variables for properties of a sum of random variables, can be seen easily for what it is; but first we need to adapt our notation to the way that returns are typically viewed in multiperiod analysis.

In multiperiod analysis, instead of calculating returns as simple percentages, we calculate returns based on logarithmic changes (geometric returns) $r(t,t+1) = Ln(P_{t+1}) - Ln(P_t)$. Over a single period, absolute returns are not all that different from geometric returns, that is, $\frac{P_{t+1} - P_t}{P_t} \approx Ln(P_{t+1}) - Ln(P_t)$. Over multiple periods, the difference between absolute and geometric returns becomes greater; making the change from absolute return to log return also has desirable technical properties. The rest looks more or less the same as before with $r \equiv r(t, t + 1) = \mu + \varepsilon(t, t + 1)$ and $\text{var}(\varepsilon(t, t + 1)) \equiv \sigma^2$. The rest is easy to show; it also helps illuminate why the change in the definition of returns helps to make our lives easier.

We start with an initial portfolio value of P_0. The cumulative return by holding the portfolio for T periods can be written in the following form: $Ln(P_T) - Ln(P_0) = r(0, T) = \sum_{t=0}^{T-1} r(t, t+1)$. The key simplification that this form buys for us is that by using log prices, the intermediate prices P_1, P_2, and so on, cancel each other out (another telescoping series) and we are left with the ending value P_T as our starting value plus the cumulative return:

$$Ln(P_T) = Ln(P_0) + \sum_{t=0}^{T-1} r(t, t+1) \quad \text{or} \quad P_T = P_0 e^{\sum_{t=0}^{T-1} r(t,t+1)} \quad \text{(continuous}$$

compounding).

To see the fallacy, we expand the component showing the sum of returns:

$$\sum_{t=0}^{T-1} r(t, t+1) = T\mu + \sum_{t=0}^{T-1} \varepsilon(t, t+1)$$

Since the variance of returns through time is assumed constant (for now) $\text{var}(\varepsilon(t, t+1)) \equiv \sigma^2$, and $\text{var}\left(\sum_{t=0}^{T-1} r(t, t+1)\right) = \sigma^2 T$. This means that the cumulative returns of a portfolio will have a total expected return of μT and a standard deviation of $\sigma\sqrt{T}$. In other words, this means that the long-run risk of a portfolio *grows* proportionately with the square root of time. If we now overlay the notion of a normal distribution on the log changes then we can write

$$Ln(V_T) - Ln(V_0) = \left(\mu - \frac{\sigma^2}{2}\right) \times T + \sigma Z\sqrt{T}$$

$$\Rightarrow V_T = V_0 e^{\left(\mu - \frac{\sigma^2}{2}\right)T + \sigma Z\sqrt{T}}$$

The variable Z denotes the number of standard deviations that a particular portfolio's path deviates from the mean. Remember, each client only gets one portfolio and one path.

The reason that the expression for portfolio changes looks a little messier under the assumption of lognormality is because if $\ln(X)$ is a random variable that is normally distributed with mean μ and variance σ^2, then the mean of X will be $e^{\mu + \frac{1}{2}\sigma^2}$, that is, the subtracted term causing the apparent messiness keeps the mean growth of the portfolio at μ.

In the workbook we will make use of multiperiod analysis. The key thing to remember is that other than the returns being defined as log changes, random variables act as before.

You'll find it useful to create the following type of calculation in your spreadsheets:

Lognormal Portfolios

Data	
V_0	100
R	0.08
Sigma	0.16
T	10
Z	−0.674

Intermediate Steps	
$A = r - sigma * sigma/2$	0.0672
$B = Z * sigma$	−0.10792

Calculations	
$C = A * T + B * square\_root(T)$	0.330726995
$D = e^C$	1.391979723
Result $(V_0 * D)$	$139.20

You may also find it useful to refer to the following minitable of standard normal cumulative probabilities in order to make better sense of the impact of different portfolio paths. As an example of how to read the table is the following statement: There is a 10 percent chance that the return outcome will be lower than −1.282 standard deviations below the mean return.

Z Value	Cumulative Probability
−2.326	1.0%
−1.960	2.5%
−1.645	5.0%
−1.282	10.0%
−1.036	15.0%
−0.842	20.0%
−0.674	25.0%
−0.524	30.0%
−0.385	35.0%
−0.253	40.0%
−0.126	45.0%
0.000	50.0%
0.126	55.0%
0.253	60.0%
0.385	65.0%

(Continued) Z Value	Cumulative Probability
0.524	70.0%
0.674	75.0%
0.842	80.0%
1.036	85.0%
1.282	90.0%
1.645	95.0%
1.960	97.5%
2.326	99.0%

Efficient Portfolios and the Capital Market Line   The notions of efficient portfolios and the capital market line are fundamental building blocks of modern portfolio theory. As they are generally covered exhaustively in introductory books on finance, we will only cover some main highlights. We will also cover some limitations associated with practical reliance on these concepts and why the financial professional needs to be wary of creating portfolios that rely too heavily on such constructions.

At its core, the notion of portfolio efficiency is a conceptual construct, although it is usually implemented as a purely technical construct. The conceptual notion is that in normal markets characterized by freely traded financial assets, prices of those assets will fluctuate randomly and will fluctuate in a way that is imperfectly correlated. If so, then in principle one could combine assets in such a way to minimize risk for a given level of expected return. That concept is the backbone of arguments underlying diversification.

In principle, a technical implementation to explicitly calculate the efficient frontier is a purely algorithmic exercise. But before getting to the practical difficulties of implementation, let me describe the algorithm.

Given the vector of expected returns on the assets and the matrix of asset covariances, the formula for calculating the efficient frontier can easily be programmed into a spreadsheet. The result is a combination of assets that minimize *variance* for a given level of expected return

Suppose there are N random returns, where the mean returns and the variances are constant through time.

$$r_1 = \mu_1 + \varepsilon_1$$
$$r_2 = \mu_2 + \varepsilon_2$$
$$r_3 = \mu_3 + \varepsilon_3$$
$$\vdots \quad \vdots \quad \vdots$$
$$r_N = \mu_N + \varepsilon_N$$

The N random returns have covariances with $\text{cov}(\varepsilon_i \varepsilon_j) \equiv \sigma_{ij}$ for all $i\&j = \{1,2, ..., N\}$. A portfolio is created by matching a set of weights w_i to the individual assets such that $\sum_{i=1}^{N} w_i = 1$. The expected return on the portfolio is then $\mu_p = \sum_{i=1}^{N} w_i \mu_i$ and the portfolio variance is given by $\sigma_p^2 = \sum_{j=1}^{N} \sum_{i=1}^{N} w_i w_j \sigma_{ij}$. For a portfolio of two assets the expected return can be written as $\mu_p = \sum_{i=1}^{N} w_i \mu_i = w\mu_1 + (1-w)\mu_2$ and the variance $\sigma_p^2 = \sum_{j=1}^{N} \sum_{i=1}^{N} w_i w_j \sigma_{ij} = w^2 \sigma_{11} + 2(1-w)w\sigma_{12} + (1-w)^2 \sigma_{22}$. Each point on the efficient frontier can be found by finding the set of portfolio weights that minimize σ_p^2 subject to a desired rate of return $\mu_p = x\%$. A depiction of the frontier is provided in Figure P.1. There is a wide variety of software available for solving this problem and graphing out the efficient frontier.

In practice the translation from concept to reality is far more difficult than most people realize. First, risk and variance are not synonyms. Variance is a two-sided concept implying gains and losses, while risk is almost always taken to mean loss. Also, except under conditions of symmetry, a distribution skewed to the downside has more risk than a distribution skewed to the upside, but they may have equal variances. Second, empirical frontiers require that there be more observations than assets, but data limitations mean that frontiers are generally calculated on small subsets of available assets. The dirtiness of the data—that can be taken to mean anything from limited data and sampling problems to nonnormality—means that the

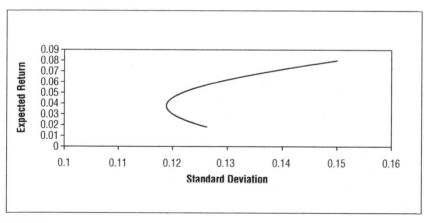

FIGURE P.1 Example of an Efficient Frontier

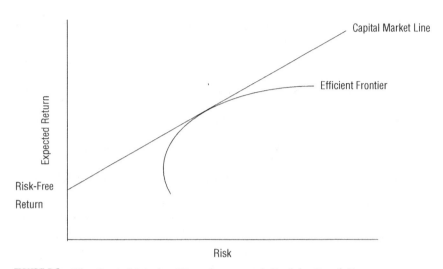

FIGURE P.2   The Capital Market Line: Conceptual Goal for Portfolios

results almost always have to be massaged to look right. The important point for our purposes is that the concept of portfolio constructions groping toward some risk versus return trade-off still resonates. When advisers put together portfolios they are generally trying to create portfolios that are as good on a risk versus return basis as possible, even if not exactly equal to mean/variance efficiency.

For our purposes the capital market line, depicted in Figure P.2, is an important concept. The capital market line represents the way that risk-free assets can be combined with risky portfolios to enable clients to find their preferred trade-off of risky and riskless assets. In its precise form, the capital market line represents the line of highest slope connecting the risk-free asset and a tangency point on the efficient frontier.

Our goal is to build portfolios for our clients that lie on the capital markets line. With investor preferences that incorporate lifestyle needs, we are generally out of the realm of mean/variance analysis; but we are still within the conceptual framework of a risk-return trade-off. The difference is that risk is no longer measured by portfolio volatility, but by the probabilities and outcomes whereby a portfolio does not meet minimum required outcomes. Risk is no less objective or quantifiable; but it is not generally found by reference to an abstract and impersonal probabilistic notion. Instead, it is the answer to a very direct question: Where does your lifestyle become imperiled?

Questions

Portfolio Focus and Stage of Life

Contents

Objectives

CHAPTER RECAP

This chapter showed that traditional portfolios, built for accumulation of wealth, frequently fail during withdrawal in retirement. In a nutshell, the problem is that traditional portfolios are designed around the principle of finding what is, on average, the best alternative—and finding the best portfolio for an individual client out of those that will not fail. These first few examples are designed to reinforce the notions that drawdown plans suffer from major weaknesses.

- When making withdrawals the order of returns matters
- The timing of retirement can have a significant impact on the likelihood of success or failure
- Unexpected shocks, even one-time shocks, can destroy a plan
- Outliving one's assets becomes a more acute risk for an "optimized" withdrawal strategy

PROBLEMS

Our purpose here is to examine what does and does not work. For simplicity, we assume throughout this chapter that each client is at the point of retirement. A secondary purpose of these problems is to gently brush away cobwebs that you may have acquired with some refresher exercises geared to the material at hand.

Problems 1–10 refer to the following set of returns data and assume that the starting portfolio value is $1,000,000:

Period	Return
1	10%
2	−10%
3	−10%
4	10%
5	−10%
6	−10%
7	−10%
8	−10%
9	−10%
10	−10%
11	−10%
12	−10%
13	10%
14	30%
15	30%
16	30%
17	30%
18	30%
19	30%
20	30%

1. Find the arithmetic average return over the 20-year sample period.
2. Find the geometric average return over the 20-year sample period.
3. For an accumulation portfolio, assume that the client, the Scott family, starts with $1 million and saves an additional $50,000 per year at the beginning of each year for each of the next 20 years. Find the value of the Scott's portfolio, assuming the return stream above, at the end of 20 years.
4. Assuming the data from Problem 3, find the geometric average of growth rate for the net increase in the Scott's portfolio value.

5. Suppose that a client, the Andrews family, wants to draw down the $1,000,000 family portfolio by $50,000 per year. Withdrawals will be made at the beginning of the year. If the Andrews put the remaining money in a checking account earning 2 percent, find whether the funds will last for 20 years.

6. Suppose that the breadwinner in the Petrocelli family is retiring and the family wants to draw down the $1,000,000 portfolio by $50,000 per year. Withdrawals will be made at the end of the period. If the Petrocellis put the money in an account comprised of the risky assets with the return stream provided in Problem 1, find whether the funds will last for 20 years or whether they come up short.

7. Another client, the Foys, have perfect foresight and know the return stream given at the start of this section will occur. To the nearest $250, find the maximum annual withdrawal that the Foys can take from the account that will be guaranteed to last for 20 years.

8. The Howard family has $1,000,000 and will invest in the risky portfolio given at the start of this section. They are willing to adjust their retirement lifestyle each year to make sure that the money lasts for 20 years. To achieve their goal, they will draw down the portfolio at the beginning of each year by 1/the remaining number of years, that is, 1/20, 1/19, 1/18, ..., 1/2, 1. Show how much the Howard family receives in income in each year.

9. Using a flat 3 percent yield curve for Treasury securities, find the present value of a 20-year annuity that pays $50,000 at the beginning of each period.

10. The Smiths want to make sure that they are covered. They purchase Treasury securities that will pay them $50,000 per year and put the rest in a portfolio that has the return stream given previously. The Treasury yield curve is flat at 3 percent. They will draw down their risky account at the beginning of each period as the Howards have done in Problem 8. Find their annual income.

Research analysts have a feeling that the next period will bring returns of 40 percent. Suppose that they are correct, but that the remaining returns for periods 2–20 are as given in the table at the start of this section.

11. Find the simple sample average return for the 20-year period assuming a 40 percent return in period 1.

12. Find the geometric average return for the 20-year period assuming a 40 percent return in period 1.

13. The Tartabull family will be drawing down $1,000,000 at $50,000 per year at the beginning of the year. Determine whether the inclusion of a 40 percent return in period 1 is sufficient to enable a successful drawdown scheme.

14. Suppose that the information is as in Problem 13, but the withdrawals are made at the end of the year. Determine whether the inclusion of a 40 percent return in period 1 is sufficient to enable a successful drawdown scheme.

15. The Tiants are not sure how long they will live. After seeing what the Smiths had planned (Problem 10) they have decided with their adviser that they will live on $50,000 per year, received at the beginning of the year. Their adviser will create $50,000 in income for them using Treasury securities and will place the unallocated funds in a risky account with the returns stream as in Problems 1–9. At the end of the 20-year period, find how much they will have left over to fund potential longevity.

Use the following information for Problems 16 and 17:
Many portfolio books concentrate on the distribution of returns, which they assume to be normal. The following will help show how prices and portfolio values evolve if returns are normally distributed, how risky returns impact portfolio values, and briefly discuss the asymmetry of the distribution of portfolio values.

16. Your client, the Lonborgs have a $1,000,000 portfolio that follows the process $V_T = V_0 e^{\left(r - \frac{\sigma^2}{2}\right)T + \sigma Z \sqrt{T}}$. They are considering whether to place their funds in a riskless asset yielding an APR of 3 percent. Find the portfolio value that would result after 20 years if they place the funds in a risk-free account. Also, find the values if they place their funds in a risky portfolio with $r = 7$ percent, $\sigma = 12$ percent, resulting in the following outcomes: Z values $Z = -1.645$, $Z = 1.645$ (corresponding to the points where 5 percent of portfolios would fall below and 5 percent would lie above if the assumed distribution is correct).

17. Suppose that you manage a $1,000,000 for your client, the Yastrzemskis. The portfolio is designed to provide an expected return of 8 percent (continuously compounded—this works out to an APR of $e^{0.08} - 1 = 8.329$ percent) with a standard deviation of 15 percent per year. Provide the expected value of the portfolio and the dollar standard deviation sixteen years from now. Discuss why the dollar standard deviation needs to be used with care if the log returns are normally distributed.

Use the following information for Problems 18 and 19:

If we make the assumption that the logarithmic returns on a portfolio are normally distributed with the portfolio starting from a value V_0, then we can find expected values, standard deviations, and create confidence intervals for future dates.

$$\text{Ln}(V_T) - \text{Ln}(V_0) = \left(r - \frac{\sigma^2}{2} \right) \times T + \sigma Z \sqrt{T}$$

$$\Rightarrow V_T = V_0 e^{\left(r - \frac{\sigma^2}{2} \right) T + \sigma Z \sqrt{T}}$$

Where $\text{Ln}(x)$ denotes the natural logarithm of x, e is the base for the natural logarithm (roughly 2.718), T is a measure of time in years, r represents the *continuously compounded* expected return (note this is a slight change in notation from the tools section), σ is the annual standard deviation (volatility) of the portfolio, and Z is a standard normal random variable. The mean and standard deviations of such processes can be found by the following:

$$\text{Expected}[V_T] = V_0 \times e^{rT}$$

$$\sigma_{V_T} = V_0 \sqrt{e^{2rT} \left(e^{T\sigma^2} - 1 \right)}$$

18. The Adairs put all of their funds (also $1,000,000) in a single U.S. Treasury strip with a yield to maturity of 4 percent per year, maturing in 16 years. Find the value of their portfolio at the end of 16 years.

19. The Joneses put all of their funds, also $1,000,000, into a portfolio that has a mean log return of 8 percent per year and a standard deviation of 20 percent per year. Find the expected value of the Jones's portfolio and the number of standard deviations down that the portfolio would endure to end up worse off than the Adair family. Assume that the log returns are normally distributed.

CHAPTER 2

The Top-Down View

A Short Primer on Economic Models of Retirement Income

Contents

Objectives

CHAPTER RECAP

This chapter showed how the accumulation portfolios conventionally associated with Modern Portfolio Theory are really special cases of more general models. In general, garden variety accumulation portfolios ignore the importance of maintaining lifestyle. Retirement income portfolios seek to provide clients with flooring and upside in a way that balances ensuring adequate outcomes while maintaining the potential for upside.

The chapter also highlights the two main classes of flooring as tradable securities versus individual contractual agreements.

- Decomposition of retirement income as floor + upside.
- Risk aversion is likely to change with wealth.
- Fully funded versus underfunded flooring.
- Monetizing mortality through risk pooling.
- Taking market risk is an oft considered alternative.
- Capital markets contracts versus insurance contracts.

PROBLEMS

For Problems 1-7 assume the following two 1-period portfolios are available:

Portfolio 1		Portfolio 2	
Probability	Return	Probability	Return
0.7	20%	0.1	70%
0.3	−20%	0.9	0%

1. Find the expected return, variance, and standard deviation for Portfolio 1

2. Find the expected return, variance, and standard deviation for Portfolio 2

3. Determine which portfolio will be preferred by a mean/variance investor. Explain why.

In addition to the portfolios given above, use the following additional information for Problems 4–7:

To keep the focus of the problems on the resulting intuition, we assume for the following clients that they have two-period lives. We assume that they have already chosen today's consumption so that their investment returns will determine the consumption that is available to them in the future. We assume that they intend to consume their final wealth (which can include consumption in the form of making a bequest—the important point is that they want to use their wealth for some purpose).

4. Assume that your client, the Andujars, are mean-variance investors, their initial investment is $100, and the Andujar's utility function is given by

the expression, $U = \text{Expected}(\text{Final wealth}) - \dfrac{\text{Variance}(\text{Final wealth})}{100}$.
Find the preferred portfolio.

5. In contrast to the previous problem, an otherwise identical client, the Hernandez family, has a floor level of consumption set at \$85. Determine the preferred portfolio for this investor.

6. Assume that the McGees' initial investment is \$100 and that their utility function is given by $U = \sqrt{\text{Final wealth}}$. Find which of the portfolios will be their preferred portfolio.

7. In contrast, assume that the Tenaces' initial investment is \$100 and their utility function is now given by $U = \sqrt{\text{Final wealth} - 80}$. Find the preferred portfolio.

8. Explain your answer to Problems 5 and 7 in terms of the concepts covered in Chapter 2.

9. Suppose that our client, the Sutter family, has a flooring need that is \$50,000 above what will be provided by Social Wealth sources. The client is 65 and flows must begin one year from today. The client is concerned about possibly living until age 105. Assume that the Treasury yield curve is flat at 4 percent. Find the amount that the client needs in order for lifestyle flooring to be considered fully funded.

The following information is used in Problems 10–14 (these Problems are mostly preliminaries for getting to a point):
Suppose that your client the Kaats have \$1,000,000 in assets and are willing to take diversified credit risk in creating an income floor. Suppose further that there are two closed-end corporate bond funds that will make level payments over some interval.

	Fund A	**Fund B**
Coverage	20 years	40 years
Level	1\$/yr	1\$/yr
Mkt Price	\$11.47	\$14.82
Annualized Volatility	0.01	0.015

The funds consist of A- and AA-rated bonds and each share will provide a level stream of \$1 per year over the coverage period.

In addition, assume that there are two diversified risky funds having the following properties:

	Risky Fund C	**Risky Fund D**
Mean Return	8%	14%
Standard Deviation	16%	24%

10. Find the cost of creating both 20-year and 40-year level flooring at $50,000 for the Kaats, and the amount of the remainder funds that can be placed in the risky funds in each of the cases.

11. Find the yield to maturity on each of the flooring funds.

12. Find the expected return and volatility (standard deviation) on portfolios comprised of 20 years of flooring and the remainder in diversified Risky Fund C.

13. Find the expected return and volatility (standard deviation) on portfolios comprised of 40 years of flooring and the remainder in the diversified Risky Fund D.

14. The portfolio with the 40-year floor has a higher mean and standard deviation than the portfolio with a 20-year floor, granted this is a hypothetical *example*, but comment on the result that the portfolio with a higher allocation to a secured floor may have more risk and higher return than a more "balanced" portfolio.

The Value of Insurance and Monetizing Mortality

15. Suppose that the Smiths are clients who have a utility function given by $U = (\text{Wealth})^{0.5}$. Given the risky portfolio used previously

| | Portfolio |
Probability	Return
0.7	20%
0.3	-20%

find the risk-free yield that would make the Smiths prefer a risk-free asset over the risky portfolio.

Use the following information to answer Problems 16–18:

Suppose that the remaining life for any and every investor is either 1 or 2 years, but that an insurance contract is available that pays $150,000 if the holder is alive and nothing if deceased. The "annuity" would cost $95,000 to purchase. There are no death benefits associated with the annuity. There is an 80 percent chance that the client will survive to receive the benefits.

16. If your client, the Lahti family's utility function is given by $U = \sqrt{\text{Final wealth}}$, determine whether they will prefer placing $95,000 in the insurance contract or in the risky asset given in Problem 15.

17. Suppose that the Sutters are clients who have a lifestyle floor of $20,000. Using the above information find the preferred portfolio. Discuss.

18. Now we add credit risk. Suppose the conditions are as in Problem 17, but that there is a 1 percent chance that the insurance product will default on the obligation. Determine the preferred portfolio and discuss.

19. Suppose that inflation rates are roughly normal such that the price level follows geometric Brownian motion of the form:

$$\text{Ln}(V_T) - \text{Ln}(V_0) = \left(r - \frac{\sigma^2}{2}\right) \times T + \sigma Z\sqrt{T}$$

$$\Rightarrow V_T = V_0 e^{\left(r - \frac{\sigma^2}{2}\right)T + \sigma Z\sqrt{T}}$$

Where $\text{Ln}(x)$ denotes the natural logarithm of x, e is the base for the natural logarithm (roughly 2.718), T is a measure of time in years, r represents the *continuously compounded* expected return, σ is the annual standard deviation (volatility) of the portfolio, and Z is a standard normal random variable. The mean and standard deviations are given by the following:

$$\text{Expected}[V_T] = V_0 \times e^{rT}$$

$$\sigma_{V_T} = V_0\sqrt{e^{2rT}\left(e^{T\sigma^2} - 1\right)}$$

Suppose that inflation averages 2 percent per year with a standard deviation of 1 percent per year. For a $100,000 standard of living in today's dollars, find the mean and standard deviation, and the outcomes for $Z = \pm1.645$ and $Z = \pm2.33$ (where the 5 percent and 1 percent upper and lower tails begin) corresponding to the same lifestyle 25 years from today. Discuss the asymmetry in inflation risk.

For Problems 20 and 21, use the following information:
Your client, the Porters, have a $1,000,000 portfolio currently invested in a well-diversified portfolio with a $\beta = 1$. Returns on the portfolio (measured by $r = \text{Ln}(P_t) - \text{Ln}(P_{t-1})$, $r = .03 + .05\beta + \varepsilon$. Suppose that the portfolio is considered well diversified enough to ignore idiosyncratic risk. The volatility of the market portfolio is 15 percent per year. For any well-diversified portfolio considered, the volatility of the portfolio is given by the following relationship $\sigma_{\text{portfolio}} = \sqrt{\beta^2\sigma_{\text{market}}^2} = .15\sqrt{\beta^2}$ per year.

20. Using the geometric Brownian motion process shown for Problem 19, find the expected value of the portfolio in 25 years, the value of the

portfolio if cumulative returns are 1 and 1.645 standard deviations below the mean, and the implied realized returns in those down states.

21. Suppose that an otherwise identical client, the Ramseys think that the expected portfolio value is insufficient to support their desired retirement lifestyle. To support current lifestyle, you show the Ramseys that the portfolio would need to grow to $10,000,000. Show the client that switching to a portfolio with β = 1.25 brings the expectation of the portfolio to $10 million but the downside is greater than before. Using the new portfolio, find the expected value of the portfolio in 25 years, the value of the portfolio if cumulative returns are 1 and 1.645 standard deviations below the mean, and the implied realized returns in those down states.

22. Discuss why the −1.645 (5 percent tail) is lower in Problem 21 even though the portfolio has a higher expected return and achieves a higher expected value than the portfolio in Problem 21.

23. Calculating how long an annuity can last—this will come in handy for the material presented in Chapter 7: Use the following formula, preferably in a spreadsheet where you can input the parameters and then create the formula

$$
N = \frac{1}{M} \left(\frac{Ln\left(1 - \frac{V}{P}\left(\frac{\frac{r}{M} - \frac{g}{M}}{1 + \frac{g}{M}}\right)\right)}{Ln\left(\frac{1 + \frac{g}{M}}{1 + \frac{r}{M}}\right)} \right)
$$

Calculate the length of time that an annuity of $100,000 can be generated from a portfolio worth $1,000,000 at the start of the process. Assume that rates are flat at 4 percent, payments are annual, and the annuity is level—that is, g = 0. Note that the formula above is for an ordinary annuity where the first payment is made one period from now.

24. Calculate the number of periods that an annuity will last for an annuity of $100,000 per year growing at 3 percent per year and with quarterly payments; rates are again flat at 4 percent.

CHAPTER 3

The Importance of Lifestyle Flooring

Contents

Objectives

Estimating the amount of flooring that is required
Anticipating the impact of inflation
Evaluating your choices in type of flooring

CHAPTER RECAP

This chapter demonstrated a way to think about the client's ability to fund consumption during retirement using the familiar tools of a balance sheet and pro forma income statements. The economics of meeting lifestyle needs sets a floor under consumption and changes the advisory framework from expectations to both outcomes and expectations. Outcomes are the important facet of flooring, and expectations are the important facet of upside. Methods useful for gauging flooring needs are covered. These range from ad hoc and unsophisticated tools such as yes/no planning to both top-down and bottom-up methods for estimating needs. Finally, the chapter circles back to the balance sheet to discuss how the client's lifestyle relative to available wealth helps to inform the adviser about the proper choice and positioning of flooring for a particular client.

Digression: Balance Sheet Template

Before beginning the problems for this chapter, it may be helpful to create a template balance sheet. This template is useful for the problems in this chapter, but more importantly, you may find it useful beyond the confines of this book:

Assets	Liabilities
Human Capital	PV of future consumption
Earnings	Preretirement
Patents	Postretirement
Entrepreneurial endeavors	
Financial Capital	PV of desired bequest
Financial portfolio	To offspring
Real assets to be monetized	To charity
Accrued DB pensions	
Social capital	Discretionary wealth
PV of Social Security income	Will equal assets less PV of
Anticipated inheritance	future consumption and any
Expected assistance (family,	desired bequest
community, etc.)	
Total	Total

Although it is unlikely that clients will know the present values of their liabilities, you may find it helpful to have clients fill out a version of a balance sheet; in the financial asset section have them note yes/no whether they plan to sell some or all of the real assets at a later date to fund their lifestyle. For entries requiring present values, it is easiest to ask them the annual flow amounts that you can be PV—at the risk-free rate.

It is an aside, but a critically important aside, that the PV of the minimum needs of the client is discounted at the risk-free rate. A person has to eat. Clients either make the payments required to maintain their consumption floor or the concept of a consumption floor has no real meaning. The cost of food, shelter, and clothing is not subject to adjustment based on the client's credit. Some aspects of the floor are somewhat subjective and personal, but they are what the client feels are absolutely necessary.

Some clients have real assets that may or may not be sold to finance lifestyle. Even if the client does not intend to sell an asset like their home, it is useful to account for the asset, but segregate its value from calculation of discretionary wealth. My preferred way to handle this is with the analog of accumulated depreciation that is used in corporate balance sheets; a contra-asset approach. Using the contra-asset approach accounts for the asset, but removes the value from consideration. An example of the balance sheet fragment relevant is as follows:

Financial Capital
- Portfolio
- House
- PV of future housing provided

PROBLEMS

1. Suppose that our clients, the Piniella family, are 15 years from retirement. The Piniellas earn $100,000 per year. Our clients have a $500,000 balanced portfolio, a $600,000 house with a balance of $350,000 and 15 years remaining on a fixed-rate mortgage. Exclusive of the mortgage payments, the client consumes $65,000 per year in after-tax necessary expenditures. The PV of preretirement expenses is $750,000. For their desired lifestyle, securing a consumption floor would cost $1,100,000, net of Social Security. The PV of future earnings is $1,750,000. Our client's discount future income flows at 4 percent. The risk-free rate is 3 percent. Social Security pays $15,000 per year beginning at age 66. Their combined federal and state marginal tax rate is 40 percent. Using the information available, calculate the Piniella's discretionary wealth and develop this client's balance sheet.

Use the following information to help answer Problems 2–12.
Suppose that it is now January 1. Our several, nearly identical 53-year-old clients each earn $100,000 per year, paid annually on the date of birth (December 31 for all of them). Retirement commences the day after turning 65. The other assets each of our clients own include a $400,000 balanced portfolio and a $1,000,000 house with a remaining mortgage of $400,000.

Exclusive of the mortgage, the clients each consume $65,000 per year in necessary expenditures. Our client's discount future income flows at 4 percent. The risk-free rate is 3 percent.

2. The Guidrys are our first client. Using the information available, calculate the Guidry's discretionary wealth and develop their balance sheet.

3. For the Nettles family, find the wealth if there is an expectation that their earnings will rise by 10 percent per year until retirement.

4. The Gossage family comes to you with a question. Using only wealth from the portfolio, find the maximum annual, fully secure income during retirement up to age 85 (assume that retirement withdrawals commence on the Mrs. Gossage's 66th birthday and end the day after her 85th birthday).

5. The Stanleys have a similar question. Using all discretionary wealth, find the maximum annual, fully secure income during retirement up to age 85 implied by the information in Problems 1 and 2 (assume that retirement withdrawals commence on Mr. Stanley's 66th birthday and end the day after his 85th birthday). The discount rate is 3 percent.

6. Suppose that an identical client, the Rivers family, tells us that $10,000 per year out of earnings is saved. Find the new balance sheet.

In addition to the previous information, Problems 7–12 take expected inflation into account.

7. Suppose that the Figueroas' inflation expectations are running at 3 percent per year. Find the inflation-adjusted cost of each dollar's worth of today's income required in 20 years and 40 years.

8. Suppose that the Munsons' inflation expectations are running at 2 percent per year. Find the risky income stream that is constant in real terms assuming discretionary wealth of $2,000,000. For the risky income stream, use a discount rate of 4 percent

9. Suppose that the Hunters want to maintain a *real* lifestyle for now and throughout retirement. Assume the conditions underlying Problem 2 and a 2 percent rate of inflation. Find the level of discretionary wealth after securing the consumption floor.

10. Referring to your answer in Problem 8, discuss the implications of the Hunters making a decision to stay in their current home.

11. Suppose that your client, the Dents, wanted to consume at a real rate of $100,000 per year (the client is willing to sell the house), inflation

is running at 2 percent per year. Determine whether such a rate of consumption is feasible.

12. Referring now to Problem 11. Suppose that the breadwinner of the client unit can defer retirement for a year. Determine whether the $100,000 real lifestyle is feasible.

The following information applies to Problems 13 and 14:
Suppose that it is now January 1st. Our 66-year-old client the Jacksons are retired with no remaining human capital. Our client's assets include a $2,000,000 portfolio and a $1,000,000 house with no mortgage.

13. Find the Jackson's base level of consumption.

14. If financial markets drop by 40 percent, find the impact on the Jackson's wealth and consumption.

15. Suppose that your client, the Chambliss family, decides to switch assets from the current choice of a balanced portfolio to a high-beta portfolio expected to earn 15 percent per year. Find the impact on the balance sheet of the Chambliss family.

16. A client with a present value of consumption that exceeds their financial wealth should be guided to an annuity. True, false, or uncertain? Explain.

17. Discuss the following proposition: A client family with a present value of consumption well below their wealth will never choose to annuitize.

CHAPTER 4

Monetizing Mortality

Annuities and Longevity Insurance

Contents

Objectives

CHAPTER RECAP

This chapter provided a light introduction to the mechanics of risk pooling and its application to the market for mortality-based payouts. The traditional range of products associated with retirement, longevity insurance, annuities, and complex annuities are covered. Most of the pros and cons of using insurance products to provide basic flooring or the more elaborate products offering flooring plus upside relate to the client's circumstances, needs, and preferences. For advisers dealing with clients about insurance it can be difficult to distinguish a client's underlying preferences from their private information about longevity.

This chapter also touched upon the credit risk associated with insurance claims. Inducing clients to place their financial assets in a debt obligation of a single entity is something about which advisers should be very cautious; it is as true of insurance as it is of corporate bonds.

PROBLEMS

1. (Warm up) Assume a 4 percent discount rate. Find the discounted value of a lump sum payment at the end of 30 years.

2. Assume that the lump sum is a longevity payment that will be received only if the client is alive. Suppose further that the client's probability of being alive to receive the claim is 30 percent. Find the value of the longevity contract.

3. Find the implied yield to maturity assuming the client's survival and the expected yield to maturity.

4. Suppose that a death benefit is attached to the longevity contract that pays the client's estate if the client dies before receiving the longevity claim. The death benefit pays 10 percent of the longevity claim payable on the same date as the longevity contract is scheduled to pay. Determine the value and yield to maturity of this contract.

5. The closest description of life expectancy is given by which of the following:
   a. The certain date of death
   b. Maximum lifetime
   c. Typical age at death
   d. The length of the average life

6. Suppose that life expectancy for someone who survives to retirement is 85 years, with a standard deviation of 6 years. Suppose further that you have a large number of retirement-age clients. Use a standard-normal distribution's 5 percent tail value of 1.645 standard units. Find the nearest age to which 5 percent of your clients will be expected to survive beyond.

7. The act of surrendering an annuity is usually costly for the client. Many of those who directly face clients in the insurance industry contend that the prospect of surrender charges inhibits sales of annuities. If surrender

charges do inhibit sales of annuities, discuss a rationale for the insurance industry to want to continue to maintain surrender charges.

Use the following information for the next three problems:
Suppose that the yield curve is a flat 6 percent. All of the debt obligations of XYZ insurance company have a very high rating. The credit spread on XYZ's debt is 30 basis points (bps).

8. *Baseline.* Find the PV of a $1,000 zero-coupon bond at the risk-free rate and at the credit-adjusted rate.

9. *Implying mortality risk.* Suppose that XYZ is offering, without markup, one-year longevity policies that pay $1,000 if the holder is still alive one year from purchase and $0 if deceased. If the policies are priced at $917.22, compare XYZ's straight debt with this policy to find the probabilities of survival or death.

10. *Implying default probabilities.* Suppose that in the event of a default by XYZ, claimants will receive 40 percent of the amount owed to them (i.e., assume a 40 percent recovery rate). Use the difference between the cost of riskless debt and XYZ's risky debt to calculate the market's implied probability of a default by XYZ.

Note: We'll spend more time on implying default probabilities using credit spreads in the problems to Chapter 5. In general, credit spreads are more informative than ratings in assessing default probabilities.

11. Suppose that your client, the Coopers, are debating whether to by an annuity with longevity protection. The annuity with protection will pay $50,000 per year while the client remains alive but has no death benefits. The annuity will cost $573,496.10. The insurance company's literature indicates that the annuity has an expected lifetime yield of 7.25 percent. The debt of the same insurance company trades in the market at a 6 percent yield to maturity for all maturities. Your client wants to know the length of survival required before the longevity protection has any value. Payments will begin one year from today. Find the minimum length of time the Coopers must survive to make purchase of the annuity beneficial relative to a purchase of an identical level payment stream covering a fixed window.

12. Suppose that the Younts purchase an annuity offering a level $50,000 annual payment stream. The client has a lifestyle of $30,000 per year in today's prices but hopes, by creating a high enough level payment, that the impact of inflation eroding lifestyle can be mitigated. Assuming

that the client fully spends each payment received, determine the number of years before the lifestyle is imperiled by inflation running at 3 percent per year. Payments will commence one year from today.

13. Use the scenario described in Problem 12 to discuss the idea that, by purchasing an annuity providing more than the initial income the clients require, the unused portion of the funds can be placed in a money market account that will keep up with inflation; thereby the client will be able to have both longevity protection and a reasonable amount of inflation protection.

CHAPTER 5

Flooring with Capital Markets Products

Contents

Objectives

Understanding how to create a floor with bonds
  Strips, zeroes, and OID bonds
  Ladders
Government vs. corporate vs. municipal bonds
  Avoid callable bonds in flooring

CHAPTER RECAP

Capital markets provide an array of products that can be used to create lifestyle flooring. The capital markets products that are the building blocks of flooring include both governmental and corporate securities. Two of the most useful products for creating capital markets–based flooring are Treasury strips and Treasury inflation-protected securities (TIPS). Both have the advantages of high liquidity and being free of credit risk. Coupon bearing bonds, both corporate and governmental can be used for flooring. The adviser needs to be wary of using callable bonds to create a client's retirement flooring.

PROBLEMS

1a. The Haas family wants to create flooring of $30,000 per year for 30 years. Find the notional amount that the client will be purchasing.

1b. Use this in tandem with Problem 1a: Supposing that the yield curve is flat at 4 percent, find the cost of providing a level flow of $30,000 in nominal annual flooring beginning one year from today and running for 30 years.

Suppose that prices of Treasury strips are given by the following rule for the sequence of annualized forward rates. Assume that the entire strip of strips is available at semiannual maturities and compounding is semiannual (Treasury strips are available with six-month maturity intervals, Feb 15 and August 15, for at least 10 years, with only the August maturities available thereafter): $Rate_{n,n+.5} = 1.5\% + 5\,bps \times (n\ periods + 1)$, for example, for the first 6 months use $.5 \times 1.55$ percent.

2. *Check.* Find the prices of Treasury strips for the next 30 years.

An important aside: If you have access to live data feeds, it is a straightforward process, using the CUSIPs, to link to the prices of Treasury strips in a spreadsheet. From this you can create a monitor for creating flooring out of the strips of any length, from a bullet to up to 30 years of flooring, for any number of clients by client age.

3. Suppose that a TIPS yielding 3 percent semiannually was selling with its original issue notional. If, over the first year the CPI (urban, not seasonally adjusted, three-month lag) indicates inflation running at 4 percent per year, find the new expected notional, coupon rate and coupon on this security.

4. Suppose that a TIPS yielding 3 percent semiannually was selling with a notional of $1,060. If, over the next year the CPI (urban, not seasonally adjusted, three-month lag) indicates *deflation* running at 4 percent, find the new notional, coupon rate and coupon on this security.

When it comes to putting a floor under a client's lifestyle, reliability trumps return; the ability of the flooring products to perform is more important than a few basis points of return. We therefore want to spend a little more time on credit risk than is typical for books geared for practitioners.

The following three problems illuminate the relationships between credit spreads, interest rates, and probabilities of default.

Suppose that the ABC Company and the DEF Company both have outstanding zero-coupon debt with exactly one year until maturity. Both are rated identically by the three major ratings agencies. The credit spread is 30 bps for ABC and 140 bps for DEF. The risk-free yield is 2 percent.

5. Find the price of one-year risk-free debt, and the prices of ABC's and DEF's debt.

6. Find the probabilities of default for both ABC and DEF implied by their credit spreads.

7. Repeat the exercise of Problem 6 but with the assumption that the risk-free yield is 6 percent. Discuss the difference in default probabilities for the two rate environments.

8. Over the business cycle, the debt of a firm may maintain a credit rating from one of the three main ratings agencies that remains unchanged. However, the credit spreads of both the reference rating (e.g., AAA) and the particular debt issue may widen or narrow by hundreds of basis points. Discuss in the context of creating flooring out of securities with credit risk.

9. Using the following formula, similar to that used in Problem 2, for calculating the discount rate for each period: $Rate_{n,n+.5} = 3.0\% + 10\,bps \times (n\ periods + 1)$, for example, for the first 6 months use $.5 \times 3.10$ percent.

Determine the cost of creating a floor paying a real $40,000 per year for your client, the Gantners. You create the flooring out of Treasury strips designed to protect against an expected inflation rate of 2 percent for 25 years. Design for payments to commence six months from today and use semiannual compounding.

10. The Molitor family is in an identical position as the Gantner family of Problem 9. The Molitors would like to know the amount and rough cost of a longevity bullet that would pay the inflation-adjusted value of $400,000 at the end of 25 years, assuming a probability of survival of 20 percent.

11. Suppose that yields are flat at 5 percent. Your 50-year-old clients, the Thomases, would like to secure $10,000 per year in capital markets flooring out to age 90. Since few debt instruments with maturities greater than 30 years are available in the liquid marketplace, determine the cost of securing the flooring today for ages 81 to 90 (inclusive) under the expectation that rates remain constant and assuming that rates fall to zero.

CHAPTER 6

Building Retirement Income Portfolios

Contents

Objectives

Create floor and upside portfolios
Building over time

CHAPTER RECAP

This chapter serves as a foundation chapter for turning the concepts of Part One into usable, recognizable, and scalable portfolios. As we cover the basics of constructing portfolios of floor plus upside, we keep the familiar context of portfolio sleeving. By using the familiar sleeving, it becomes clearer that a small change in practice can lead to portfolios that have profoundly better outcomes for retirees. To help illustrate the process, basic portfolio constructs that we call the brick layer, track layer, and surge maker are used to help simplify how to bring retirement income into a standard adviser's practice. We end the chapter with some tips for locating retirement assets within different accounts subject to differing tax rules.

PROBLEMS

Use the following information for Problems 1–6:

The breadwinner for a client family, Mr. Ortiz, has just turned 35. He wants to create an IRA savings plan and portfolio—alongside of an ordinary portfolio—that will provide for retirement but will also provide ample potential for upside. Treasury strips paying on the day that this client turns 65 are available with a yield to maturity of 5.51 percent. Assume that the expected return on the risky subportfolio that the client prefers is 10 percent.

1. Find the cost, the IRA portfolio weights, and the IRA portfolio's expected return if the Ortiz family will save $5,000 per year in the IRA and wants to secure $10,000 in notional flooring each year.

    Suppose that the portfolio grows lognormally (Ln),

    $$Ln(V_T) - Ln(V_0) = \left(r - \frac{\sigma^2}{2}\right) \times T + \sigma Z \sqrt{T}$$

    $$\Rightarrow V_T = V_0 e^{\left(r - \frac{\sigma^2}{2}\right)T + \sigma Z \sqrt{T}}$$

    where T is some number of years from today, r represents the *continuously compounded* expected return, σ is the annual standard deviation (volatility) of the portfolio, and Z is a standard normal random variable. The mean and standard deviations of such processes can be found by the following:

    $$Expected[V_T] = V_0 \times e^{rT}$$

    $$\sigma_{V_T} = V_0 \sqrt{e^{2rT}\left(e^{T\sigma^2} - 1\right)}$$

    Note: An important technicality is that the preceding formula assumes continuous compounding. Therefore, if the annual yield is expected to be 10 percent, then the proper r to use in this equation will keep $e^r = 1.10 = 1 + 10$ percent, that is, $r_{continuous} = Ln(1.10) = .09531$. (People often forget the impact of this compounding effect and end up fooling themselves about how good the future looks.)

2. Find the expected value of the first IRA contribution to the risky portfolio and the total value of the first year's deposit into the IRA at the end of 30 years.

3. (Easy) Suppose that the Ortizes expect to stick to this plan for 30 years and that the yield curve is flat at 5.51 percent. Find the expected level

and coverage of flooring if the client will also be eligible to receive about $12,000 per year in Social Security income. Discuss why this floor is only an expectation.

4. Compute the amount expected in the risky portfolio at the end of 30 years. Assume that the client will not make a deposit on the 65th birthday, so that the last deposit is made at age 64.

5. Find the future value of the IRA flooring account and find the total expected in the IRA at the end of the 30-year savings plan, again assuming that no deposit is made after age 64.

6. Suppose that based on their current lifestyle, you reckon the client can get by on $22,000 but would ideally consume around $50,000 during retirement. Find the draw rate on the discretionary wealth portfolio expected to be required to achieve total consumption at the initial retirement level of $50,000.

7. Assuming that thirty years from now the federal tax rate equals 40 percent, find the after tax value of the $38,000 withdrawn from the IRA at age 65.

For Problems 8–10, assume that instead of the previous retirement plan, another client family, the Nixons, saved all retirement contributions, totaling $5,000 per year, in a risky portfolio.

8. Find the continuous return that would be equivalent to the annual return of 8.204 percent used in Problem 1.

9. Suppose that the Nixon's risky portfolio has an expected continuous return equal to the solution of Problem 7. Find the expected portfolio value at the end of 30 years of following the savings plan.

10. Using the expected portfolio value after 30 years, as given by the solution to Problem 9, find the drawdown rates commensurate with consuming at $10,000 and $38,000.

For Problems 11–16, use the following information:
Instead of creating IRAs, these clients will save into a fully taxable account. Assume tax rates are permanently fixed at 40 percent for ordinary income and 10 percent on capital gains. In these problems, we focus on the flows associated with the first year of saving and the first year of retirement.

11. Find the pretax earnings required to save $5,000 on an after-tax basis per year.

12. Suppose that the Variteks purchase $10,000 notional of Treasury strips maturing in 30 years and will pay taxes out of the notional. Find the after-tax notional that will remain if the pretax yield on the strips is 5.51 percent.

13. Find the notional of the strips necessary to produce $10,000 in after-tax income 30 years from now. Discuss why the answer is more than $10,000/.6.

14. Repeat the exercise in Problem 13, only this time find the amount of gross earnings necessary to build a floor with an equivalent payout to the floor from the tax deferred account.

15. Find the expected value of the after-tax income to be derived from the Schillings placing $3,000 in a nondividend, static portfolio, risky account with a continuous return of .09531 and left there for 30 years.

16. Find the amount that the Martinez family would have to save in the taxable risky portion of the account to achieve equivalence with the taxed-as-ordinary-income expectation from the risky portion of a tax-deferred account, assuming that the client sells the assets on the 30-year mark.

For Problems 17–18, use the following information:
Instead of creating traditional IRAs, these clients will save into a Roth IRA account—after-tax income on the way into the account, but tax exempt thereafter. Assume tax rates are permanently fixed at 40 percent for ordinary income and 10 percent on capital gains.

17. Suppose that the Wakefields want to match the after-tax income of the flooring account from the traditional IRA with the after-tax income of the flooring account in a Roth IRA. Find the amount that the client would need to earn for the first year's flooring and the amount that the client would need to deposit in the Roth IRA to purchase the flooring component 30 years out.

18. Suppose that the Embrees want to match the after-tax income of the upside account in the traditional IRA, with the after-tax income of the upside account in a Roth IRA. Find the amount that the client would need to earn for the first year's upside and the amount that the client would need to deposit in the Roth IRA to purchase the flooring component 30 years out.

19. Discuss how preferences for a Traditional IRA or a Roth IRA would be influenced by expectations about future tax rates.

20. Suppose that the retirement consumption of the Lowes has a present value $500,000 higher than the current portfolio value, with retirement scheduled to begin in 20 years. The client has an accumulation portfolio not currently geared to retirement income. Suppose that the risk-free rate is 3 percent, and the expected minimum of the average geometric rate of return on the client's risky portfolio is 4 percent per year. Find the amount that the client will need to save each year to have the minimum expectation exceed the underfunded gap. Assume that the client can make a deposit today, thus making a total of 21 payments.

21. Discuss the risks of using an expected or even a historical minimum geometric rate of return.

22. Suppose that the cost of a mortality-monetizing annuity providing sufficient funds to cover the consumption gap for the Bellhorns, in the same circumstances as the Lowe's in Problem 20, is currently $400,000. The Bellhorns can either purchase the annuity now or they can pay a small fee to the insurance company that would provide the annuity to lock in a price with no purchase commitment of $773,500 in 20 years. The Bellhorns are able to save $30,000 to put toward retirement. Assume that the client puts the funds in a risky portfolio. Find the minimum rate of growth that the client needs to attain sufficient funds to purchase the annuity as a fall-back position; also find the implicit rate of growth in the annuity cost.

Creating Allocations for Constructing Practical Portfolios by Age and Lifestyle Needs

Contents

Objectives

Providing usable allocations and allocation methodology for creating
    actual portfolios
Adjusting allocations for lifestyle, age, anticipated inflation, and
    life expectancy

CHAPTER RECAP

This is one of the keystone chapters of the book. First, we break the portfolio down into four components: lifestyle flooring, longevity, precautionary, and discretionary. By using the simple algebra of present values, we can create usable allocations for building retirement income portfolios that have a solid floor, protect against longevity, take precaution against the uninsurable, and provide upside opportunities. The two key parameters for driving the allocations are years until retirement and desired lifestyle. Other influential parameters include the fears of inflation, potential for longevity, and willingness to take precaution with a portion of the funds. Note that the problems for this chapter form a running theme and are, for the most part, cumulative. It will be helpful for you to work the problems in order, checking your answers as you go.

Digression: Habit Formation and Lifestyle

Asking clients about their desired level of consumption during retirement is an exercise in frustration. In simplistic portfolios, it can lead the adviser to create a portfolio that exposes the client to greater lifestyle risk.

The object is to pin down the amount that the client needs for minimum lifestyle maintenance, mentally placing the funding for all of the frills of the lifestyle into the upside part of the portfolio. With the necessities pinned down the adviser still has to cope with the likelihood that the client will want a plan that is flexible enough to accommodate a higher lifestyle down the road. Anecdotally, lower initial floors seem to become more palatable to clients if growth is built into the floor. Thus clients become either more confident about being able to keep up with inflation or willing to defer for what they ultimately desire.

Lifestyles may change for many reasons, but one of the main reasons for a change in lifestyle is a permanent change in wealth. Lifestyles tend to evolve with wealth—people get used to living in a certain style and as their wealth increases, the new lifestyle becomes the new floor. The appendix to the text goes through a model of habit formation. For many, the rise in lifestyle needs may be negligible for a range of wealth but involve jumps at various hurdles. But suffice it to say that as your client's wealth increases their tastes will likely change and what were not necessities previously will become necessary.

The easiest way to incorporate changing lifestyles programmatically is to treat the flow of consumption (floor) as a percentage of the stock of wealth. We will also create enough flexibility so that changing the flooring as a percentage of wealth is virtually costless for you in time or effort (although the client may incur transactions costs).

Creating a business model that is flexible enough for the client and simple enough for scale economies is straightforward if the floor is referenced as a proportion of wealth. Once the floor is translated to a proportion of wealth the problem becomes a problem of pure engineering; anything that can be engineered can be mass produced.

Once the flooring allocations are settled, the remaining allocations such as what I am calling longevity but may include many types of insurance protection such as long-term care, precautionary balances, and the upside portfolio become fairly straightforward.

Over the next few problems, we construct the engineering machinery necessary for you or even your assistants to fill the orders within the template you create.

PROBLEMS

1. Suppose that the Evans family is a client five years from retirement. Your client needs $100,000 per year. Find the present value of an annuity that makes its first payment five years *from today* and makes annual payments for 25 years. Assume that the yield curve is a constant 5 percent.

   Problems 2–6 will help develop a tool for determining the feasibility of client desires.

2. Suppose that your client, the Castillo family, wants you to estimate how long the portfolio (well, only a part of the portfolio, but we'll get to that) can be made to last under alternative assumptions about draw rates. Suppose to baseline the result the client asks about creating an 8 percent level draw rate, with annual withdrawals and assuming yields remain flat at 5 percent.

3. Now we'll build a column showing how long an annuity can last for different draw rates. Assume that the yield to maturity used for discounting the annuity is 5 percent. Create a column for percentage draw rates from 5 percent to 15 percent. Note that at a draw rate at or below the yield to maturity the annuity would never be depleted.

4. The next step is to turn the column into a table allowing for percentage draw rates to vary by row and creating different columns to accommodate different growth rates. Create a table allowing for draw rates of 5 percent to 15 percent and growth rates of 0 percent to 6 percent.

   Before constructing the table, we remind the reader of the special case where $r = g$ and the naïve application of the formula provides a result that is undefined. The correct answer in the undefined case is to set the result to V/P. The statement would be if($r = g$, V/P, formula), which can be read as if $r = g$, then use V/P, otherwise use the formula.

5. Not all clients are at the point of retirement. In order to make this more usable, the next step is to make the table dynamic by allowing for an input of a deferral period. If there is a deferral of D periods before the annuity, then we need to adapt the formula slightly.

$$V = P \left(\frac{1 + \dfrac{g}{M}}{1 + \dfrac{r}{M}} \right)^{DM} \left[\frac{1 + \dfrac{g}{M}}{\dfrac{r}{M} - \dfrac{g}{M}} \left(1 - \left(\frac{1 + \dfrac{g}{M}}{1 + \dfrac{r}{M}} \right)^{NM} \right) \right]$$

$$N = \frac{1}{M} \left(\frac{\mathrm{Ln}\left[1 - \dfrac{V}{P\left(\dfrac{1 + \frac{g}{M}}{1 + \frac{r}{M}} \right)^{DM}} \left(\dfrac{\frac{r}{M} - \frac{g}{M}}{1 + \frac{g}{M}} \right) \right]}{\mathrm{Ln}\left(\dfrac{1 + \frac{g}{M}}{1 + \frac{r}{M}} \right)} \right)$$

Keep in mind that the annuity is an ordinary annuity and that by construction, if the deferral is D years, then the first payment is $D + 1$ years forward.

Construct tables that replicate Problem 4, but allow for deferrals of 5 and 10 years respectively, that is, first payment in 6 and 11 years. *Hint:* Where the formula refers to the draw rate, replace with the draw rate adjusted for deferral.

6. Suppose your client is the 45-year-old breadwinner of the Garbey family with a $1,000,000 portfolio. The client wants to know that by the time he retires, his portfolio can support an inflation-adjusted $60,000 lifestyle for 30 years. Suppose that the client is worried that inflation will be running at 3 percent. Assume that the yield curve is flat at 5 percent. Find the answer to the client's question and discuss whether there is reason for optimism.

Problems 7–15 help you to develop usable allocation tables for clients:

Flooring

7. The easiest way to begin developing allocation tables for clients is to work in a spreadsheet beginning with the notional flows that are needed in each year.

   Our columns will be the ages of clients today and the rows will be the cash flows that occur during retirement. In the workbook, we use the convention that retirement occurs at age 65, although it is a straight-forward task to make all entries relative to the length of time to go until retirement.

   With columns running from age 35 to 75 at five-year increments, create a table for a 1 percent payment as a percent of current portfolio value, growing at 3 percent beginning either at age 65 or the current age of the client if greater than 65. Assume that payments start at age 65 (or at date of inception if 70 or 75). For the workbook, we truncate payments at age 100.

8. We now want to construct a table of prices (or PV factors) for the desired flows. For the workbook, we use a flat discount rate of 5 percent. Find the table of PV factors corresponding to the table created for Problem 7.

9. We now complete the first stage of our task by multiplying the entries from Problems 7 and 8. This table provides the cost per period in terms of percentage of the portfolio that would need to be allocated in order to secure flooring for each percentage of the current portfolio with 3 percent growth and yield to maturity of 5 percent.

10. If Problem 9 shows how to create the cost per period for securing each percentage of current wealth as flooring, then the total allocation required to create a floor that covers a span of years can be found by summing the per period costs to cover the desired window.

    Use the table from Problem 9 to create portfolio allocations that will secure flooring for ages 35, 40, 45, 50, 55, 60 covering from ages 65 to 80, 85, 90, 95, and 100. Determine the level of current wealth that the flow of payments will achieve.

11. Use the technology you've created to find the allocation of the current portfolio required for a 45-year-old client representing the Parrish family to set a floor at 5 percent of current wealth covering ages 65 to 85 assuming yield to maturity of 4 percent and a growth rate of 1 percent.

Longevity

12. Without mortality credits: Extend your tables and find the cost of a 1 percent allocation to flooring up to age 105. We do this because in the latter part of retirement the combination of temporal distance and the likelihood of mortality make longevity insurance, either as a bullet payment or as a deferred annuity, a highly compelling way to serve the client's needs.

Although the actual probabilities that an insurance company would be interested in involve the joint probability of surviving to time $T + 1$ given alive at period T multiplied by the probability of survival to T, such as surviving to 87 given still alive at 86 times the probability of surviving to 86.

13. Assume that the probability of survival until the start of the longevity sum is 50 percent, and that clients who survive until the protection starts are entitled to the entire stream. Find the cost of longevity protection for Mr. and Mrs. Petry, 45-year-old clients who desire a floor at 5 percent of current wealth with a growth rate of 1 percent where the longevity protection begins at age 86. The yield to maturity is 4 percent.

Overall Allocations

14. Suppose that your clients, the Johnsons, are comfortable with 5 percent of wealth in precautionary balances. Since the bulk of the client's assets will be in liquid capital markets products, the client's employment appears secure, and the client has all of the usual personal insurance, you do not advise a higher precautionary balance. For these 45-year-old clients, find the final allocation combination:

    Flooring:

    Longevity:

    Precautionary: 5 percent

    At risk:

15. Suppose that the Gibsons, 50-year-old clients, schedule an appointment to discuss transitioning the current accumulation portfolio, which is allocated 60/30/10 (equity/fixed income/cash) to a retirement income portfolio. Assume that the yield curve is flat at 6 percent, the client wants to secure flooring at 4 percent of financial wealth, expects inflation to run at 2 percent per year, and has a probability of survival past 90 of 20 percent. Determine the initial allocations for this client.

Flooring:

Longevity:

Precautionary: 5 percent

At risk:

Discuss how you would accomplish the transition.

16. Suppose that rates are 5 percent and inflation is expected to run at 3 percent. You have 65-year-old clients, the Scherrers, with flooring needs to draw at a rate of 7 percent of current wealth. Find the allocations derived from the tables and discuss the feasibility of the solution.

Allocation and Age

17. Suppose that you have a 45-year-old client representing the Lemon family. Your client wants to know the benefit of transitioning to a retirement income posture sooner rather than later. Using a 2 percent rate of anticipated inflation a 6 percent yield curve, show your client how the flooring allocation required for creating a floor lasting out to age 90 at 4 percent of assets will become more lifestyle focused as the client ages.

   Note: We will use the technology developed in Chapter 8, so you may want to keep this handy.

18. Suppose that you have a 40-year-old client who represents the Lopezes. Her lifestyle indicates that there are no feasible allocations using capital markets products: This client is underfunded. Discuss the potential for using an annuity to create potential for upside.

CHAPTER 8

Rebalancing Retirement Income Portfolios

Contents

Objectives
The importance of rebalancing rules and how they differ for the retirement income problem
Ratcheting floors and habit formation

CHAPTER RECAP

The essential feature of rebalancing for retirement income is to treat the floor as sacred. One can rebalance to add flooring, but one of the main tenets of retirement income is that the floor is not placed at risk. The net effect of the importance of the floor is to imply that rebalancing rules become one sided. One-sided rebalancing rules stand in contrast to the two-sided rebalancing rules of accumulation portfolios that tilt funds toward the underperforming components of the portfolio. Two-sided rebalancing can cause a cascade of declines persisting during withdrawals, where the effects become catastrophic.

PROBLEMS

For Questions 1–2 use the following information:
Suppose that an ordinary portfolio is constructed to have 60 percent equity and 40 percent fixed income. Suppose that equity markets have two

down years in a row with returns of −20 percent and −30 percent, respectively, while fixed-income markets are flat at 5 percent in both years. The initial value of the portfolio is $1,000,000:

1. Without rebalancing, find the value of the portfolio at the end of the second year.
2. If the portfolio is rebalanced to target at the end of each year, find the value of the portfolio at the end of the second year.

For Problems 3–6, use the following information:
Suppose that two portfolios, one an accumulation portfolio and the other a retirement income portfolio, are constructed to have 70 percent equity and 30 percent fixed income. The initial value of either portfolio is $1,000,000. The accumulation portfolio adds $50,000 per year and the retirement income portfolio withdraws $50,000 per year. The rate of return on the fixed-income portion of the portfolio is assumed constant at 5 percent.
Equity returns are given by the following table:

Period	Equity Return
1	−20%
2	−45%
3	5%
4	7%
5	−11%
6	−10%
7	10%
8	8%
9	−10%
10	7%
11	−10%
12	−10%
13	10%
14	30%
15	5%
16	10%
17	30%
18	7%
19	30%
20	10%

3. For an accumulation portfolio, find the ending value of the portfolio assuming that the client does not rebalance.

4. For an accumulation portfolio, find the ending value of the portfolio assuming that the client rebalances after each period. Discuss which method is likely to lead to the higher portfolio value in accumulation.

5. For a decumulation (retirement) portfolio, find the time to failure without rebalancing.

6. With rebalancing, find the time to failure for the portfolio given above.

For Problems 7–10, use the following information:

Suppose that you build a portfolio for a 40-year-old client based on the following allocation to flooring: $6\% \times \text{Wealth} \times \sum_{i=\text{Age }66}^{\text{Age }90} \left(\frac{1}{1.05}\right)^i$.

Assume the client has an initial wealth of \$1,000,000. The sequence of returns that will occur is the following:

Age	Risky Portfolio Return	Fixed-Income Return
40	−0.048%	5.000%
41	0.510%	5.000%
42	18.579%	5.000%
43	−13.918%	5.000%
44	−11.050%	5.000%
45	3.428%	5.000%
46	17.559%	5.000%
47	5.403%	5.000%
48	19.584%	5.000%
49	16.246%	5.000%
50	20.510%	5.000%
51	−13.515%	5.000%
52	−14.589%	5.000%
53	19.673%	5.000%
54	33.834%	5.000%
55	16.101%	5.000%
56	−6.741%	5.000%
57	18.290%	5.000%
58	16.305%	5.000%
59	−8.174%	5.000%

7. Show the client the target allocations from today through age 59 (20 years' worth) for creating the 6 percent floor with the first payment at age 66 and running up through age 89.

8. Using the allocations developed for Problem 7 and the preceding returns, show the equity allocations, the flooring allocations, and

portfolio values for each period of the client's age of 40 to 59 assuming annual rebalancing to the target allocations.

9. Show the equity allocations, the flooring allocations, and portfolio values for each period of the client's age of 40 to 59 assuming *one-sided* annual rebalancing to the target allocations.

10. Show the amount of flooring that has been gained by rebalancing in the one-sided regime.

CHAPTER 9

Active Risk Management for Retirement Income Portfolios

Contents

Objectives

Actively managing the risk of retirement income portfolios
How to manage for both safety and growth

CHAPTER RECAP

Active risk management allows creating a business model around the notion of seeking maximum exposure to upside while standing ready to protect the floor. Instead of creating static portfolios for retirement income, some advisers may build business models centered on the active risk management of client accounts. Even clients who prefer to make their own portfolio decisions can benefit from someone who can monitor and more importantly act when action is required. Whether in a transaction-based or discretionary account, an underutilized selling point of financial professionals is that they can be counted on to act when triggers are hit.

Several techniques for the risk management of client portfolios are discussed within the chapter. The rules for risk management can vary from naïve simple stops to more fluid techniques for managing risk. The important concepts to remember from the chapter relate to monitoring the portfolio cushion and taking action before the cushion falls below zero.

Digression: But They're Not Normal

Every textbook on investment analysis relies heavily on the normal and/or lognormal distributions. In some cases, like the large sample properties of sampling historical portfolio means, the model is precise and correct. In other cases, such as assuming that future returns on a particular portfolio will be normally distributed, the model may illuminate but should be used with caution. Teaching courses on investments is much easier using the neat results that fall out of well-behaved distributions, but using the easy-to-teach distributions imposes a cost in terms of practicability. Having taught investment analysis to undergraduate and graduate students, it was very easy to teach out of textbooks that focused on the neat results and clean algebra falling out of well-defined problems. However, since portfolio values and returns aren't just collections of well-behaved random variables, they are the derived effect of the behavior of individuals. When individuals change their behavior, the entire distributions of prices and returns may change; sometimes in a way that looks anything but well behaved.

In risk management, traders would frequently ask what I thought was the worst that could happen to their position. The answer was always "who knows, but how have you hedged the risk?" The real issues in front of the trader were whether a hedge was in place or if not, would a hedge be available under all market conditions; if a hedge was in place, what conditions could cause the hedge to fail. Probabilities of events and likely movements are hard to estimate; a focus on outcomes across events is often far more useful for games where there is a single play.

"That was a 10-standard deviation event." I've heard that line too many times. Not counting the events of late 2008, I've heard it applied to commodity prices, credit spreads, currencies, real estate, stock prices, and even boring old Treasury securities. They happen a lot more frequently than the normal distribution would imply—which, irrespective of the differences in beliefs about creation, would be roughly once since the universe was created. So what can one say with confidence? If the normal distribution provides the lower bound odds of some bad event with a well-behaved distribution, then maybe we need to put an upper bound on the odds for cases where the distribution is not so well behaved.

All of the above being said, it is still useful to use the distributions like the normal distribution, particularly if we use it as the best case model. If the normal distribution—the best case—indicates that a portfolio construction has some cause for concern, then we should be doubly wary of such constructions, particularly for retirement where the client gets no do-over.

But what if the normal distribution indicates that there should be no worries? That's when the Dr. Doom in me likes to trot out the Chebychev inequality. What the Chebychev inequality tells us is that if we don't want to make any assumptions about the underlying probability distribution for prices or returns or whatever, then all we can say is that the probability of a N-sigma event is at most $1/N^2$. This means that 10-sigma events can happen at most 1 percent of the time. Unlike the normal distribution, Chebychev doesn't assume symmetry, so one needs to interpret the Chebychev results as two-tailed estimates of probability bounds; depending on the outcome space, Chebychev bounds may include some very good outcomes alongside of very bad outcomes. Between the two extremes of Normal (immeasurably remote possibility) and Chebychev (not so unlikely), the truth can be found.

Bad things can happen to good portfolios. The active management of risk has less to do with trying to precisely estimate probabilities than avoiding severe outcomes.

PROBLEMS

Passive Risk Management

1. The one-sided rebalancing plan covered in Chapter 8 is an example of passive risk management. Discuss the proposition that such a risk management program will have the highest drag on a portfolio in steadily rising markets.

2. Using discrete portfolio high-water marks to raise flooring is a variation on one-sided rebalancing. Under simple one-sided rebalancing, the client portfolio is rebalanced back to target allocations every time that the portfolio hits a new high-water mark—a narrow window. Under discrete high-water mark rebalancing, flooring would only be incremented when the risky portfolio exceeds a threshold amount—a wider window. The selling point of the discrete plan is that it allows the risky portfolio to run for a while before reallocating some of the gains to flooring. Discuss which method would work best under whipsaw market conditions and which would work best in markets with persistence.

Cushion

Use the following information for questions 3–5:

Suppose that you observe the following set of prices for Treasury Principal Strips:

Maturity in Years	Price
1	$99.04
2	$96.87
3	$94.54
4	$90.28
5	$86.49
6	$83.40
7	$76.94
8	$73.00
9	$69.79
10	$65.74
11	$60.36
12	$57.05
13	$54.04
14	$51.23
15	$48.96
16	$46.91
17	$45.38
18	$42.68
19	$41.16
20	$39.60
21	$38.28
22	$36.59

Maturity in Years	Price
23	$35.56
24	$34.40
25	$33.11
26	$31.83
27	$30.63
28	$30.18
29	$29.46
30	$28.78

3. Suppose that the head of the Dravecky family is your 55-year-old client who wants to retire in four years. A deferred annuity that will begin payments at age 85 has already been purchased. The client wants to know the current cost of buying $80,000 per year in flooring to cover ages 60 through 84. Payments will cover years 5 through 29 in the table. The client has a total portfolio of $1.5 million. Find the client's cushion.

4. Suppose that your client the Garvey family desires higher exposure to risky assets than the amount implied by the previous problem. You tell the client that there is a way to manage the risk such that more than the cushion is exposed to risk, but that your vigilance will ensure that no more than the cushion can be lost. Given the client's age and risk appetite, you suggest a multiplier of 2, explaining to the client that if the risky portfolio were to fall by 50 percent, the cushion would be gone but the flooring would still be secure. On the upside, you explain that given the higher exposure to risk it will be more readily possible to take advantage of up moves. Find the client's initial allocation to flooring and exposure to risky assets with a multiplier of 2.

5. Suppose another one of your clients, the Mota family, is interested in the proposition you put forth in Problem 4. However, the client only wants you to be rebalancing once a quarter (unless something drastic happens). Discuss the impact of quarterly, or infrequent, rebalancing on the cushion and the impact on the amount of risky exposure that you will place on behalf of the client. *Hint:* Consider the cost of flooring.

Use the following data for Problems 6–8:

Suppose that the risky portfolio exhibits the following returns over the next six years and that the cost of the flooring changes according to the following table:

Quarters	Risky Return	Flooring Price Changes
1	1.70%	0.80%
2	4.66%	1.09%
3	−3.39%	0.98%
4	6.12%	1.00%
5	−9.92%	0.92%
6	7.23%	0.97%
7	0.97%	0.96%
8	1.82%	1.01%
9	−2.72%	0.81%
10	0.38%	0.99%
11	−0.59%	0.80%
12	2.67%	1.00%
13	−9.51%	0.88%
14	1.64%	1.17%
15	−9.87%	1.20%
16	1.99%	1.01%
17	−5.25%	0.82%
18	12.31%	0.99%
19	13.91%	0.99%
20	2.86%	1.07%
21	−8.65%	1.01%
22	1.67%	0.85%
23	1.26%	0.94%
24	6.45%	1.00%

6a. Find the cumulative return of $100 in the risky portfolio and $100 in flooring costs.

6b. If the costs of flooring are rising faster than the risky portfolio, discuss the impact of active risk management strategies on the cumulative portfolio value.

7. Find the cost of flooring, cushion, allocations to flooring and risky assets, and the portfolio values under the assumption that you will manage the cushion to provide fully for the flooring cost each period. For now ignore that the client will be withdrawing funds during retirement, which begins in 16 quarters.

8. Using a multiplier of 2, and using the exact cushion as calculated in Problem 4, find the client's allocations and portfolio values assuming the returns and flooring cost changes provided in the preceding table. As with Problem 7 ignore the client's withdrawals for now.

Use the following data for Problems 9–12:

We will create some "lucky" data for the next series of problems. To make your life easier, we create the lucky data by adding 125 bps (.0125) to each of the returns in the risky returns series of the previous data set. Hopefully, if you've input the data into a spreadsheet, the change will be straightforward and easier than typing in new data. For the sake of clarity, I display the new data below:

Quarter	Risky Return	Flooring Price Changes
1	2.95%	0.80%
2	5.91%	1.09%
3	–2.14%	0.98%
4	7.37%	1.00%
5	–8.67%	0.92%
6	8.48%	0.97%
7	2.22%	0.96%
8	3.07%	1.01%
9	–1.47%	0.81%
10	1.63%	0.99%
11	0.66%	0.80%
12	3.92%	1.00%
13	–8.26%	0.88%
14	2.89%	1.17%
15	–8.62%	1.20%
16	3.24%	1.01%
17	–4.00%	0.82%
18	13.56%	0.99%
19	15.16%	0.99%
20	4.11%	1.07%
21	–7.40%	1.01%
22	2.92%	0.85%
23	2.51%	0.94%
24	7.70%	1.00%

9. Using the new data, and ignoring the retirement date, find the allocations and portfolio values corresponding to a multiplier of 1.

10. With a multiplier of 2 repeat the exercise. Determine the maximum value of the portfolio if the multiplier is increased to 4. Interpret and discuss this result.

11. Before we get to the retirement withdrawals, we have one last change to make: Our client, the Sutton family, wants to create a mechanism

to take money off the table if the portfolio has more cushion than required to obtain 100 percent exposure to risky assets. Determine the changes required to accomplish this feature. Use a multiplier of 3 to check your results.

12. A similar client to the Suttons of Problem 11, the John family is only 16 quarters from retirement; we now want to adjust the portfolio for withdrawals of $20,000 + (Portfolio − Cost of Remaining Flooring) × (1/Remaining Periods), that is, 1/100, 1/99, 1/98.... The withdrawals begin at the end of period 17. Use a multiplier of 2 and show how the portfolio evolves.

13. Discuss the feasibility of active risk management for a client whose portfolio value is below the present value of flooring costs.

Use the following information to answer Problems 14 and 15:

Suppose that the breadwinner of the Gossage family, a 50-year-old client, has a portfolio valued at $1,000,000 and a present value of retirement consumption of $1,120,000. Assume that the client is willing to accept an annuitization solution at age 65 as a second-best solution if the portfolio grows insufficiently to cover the present value of consumption with room for upside. Assume further that an annuity covering the client's needs can be purchased for $850,000 if purchased today. Assets that are not allocated to the risky portfolio will be placed in a cash account yielding 2 percent. By the time the client retires, the present value of consumption will have grown to $1,622,094.

For Problems 14 and 15, use the following data to determine whether your client will need to annuitize:

Age	Risky Return	Increase in Annuity Costs
50	−5.110%	3.640%
51	−5.640%	4.930%
52	18.370%	3.270%
53	−20.610%	3.500%
54	21.150%	1.750%
55	27.770%	2.170%
56	28.240%	5.070%
57	16.430%	4.320%
58	9.890%	4.770%
59	33.030%	3.430%
60	14.070%	3.350%
61	6.900%	3.160%
62	2.950%	4.310%

Age	Risky Return	Increase in Annuity Costs
63	29.800%	3.450%
64	8.440%	3.660%
65	22.670%	1.720%

14. Suppose that the costs of the annuity rise by a fixed 3.5 percent per year. Rebalancing is conducted annually. Determine whether the Bevacqua family, your client, will need to annuitize.

15. Per the provided table, suppose the costs of the annuity will rise randomly but at a mean of around 3 percent. Rebalancing will only take place annually. Setting the effective cushion to reflect the actual flooring costs adjusted for the average increase in the cost of the annuity, determine whether your client will need to annuitize.

The Transition Phase

Contents

Objectives

Moving clients from an accumulation portfolio into retirement
    income portfolios
Keeping clients on the path to their goals
Making it all feel natural

CHAPTER RECAP

Transitions can be abrupt or prolonged. The earlier in a client's life that the portfolio is tilted toward retirement income, the easier it is to create a retirement portfolio, or begin the process of readying the client for a product geared for their retirement, rather than waiting and trying to sell the unwanted to the unwilling. This chapter shows how to avoid abrupt changes and turn the transition "problem" around to create a natural evolution that can strengthen the relationship with the client.

PROBLEMS

1. Discuss what is the earliest practical date to begin working on transitioning a client's accumulation portfolio to a retirement income portfolio.

2. Suppose your client has just changed employers. Discuss the opportunity to create a retirement income transition using the client's assets in the former employer's sponsored plan.

The natural point to engage in a transition from accumulation to retirement income focus is when the allocation to fixed income in the accumulation portfolio equals the allocation to flooring that would be obtained in a retirement income portfolio.

Use the following information for Problems 3–5:

Assume that rates are 5 percent and expected inflation is 2 percent. Cash flows are to begin at age 66.

3. Suppose that the Shelby family is your client. They have an accumulation portfolio with a 60/30/10 allocation to equity, fixed income, and cash. Find the "natural" date to begin transitioning the client's portfolio to a retirement income focus. Assume the flooring level is 4 percent of financial wealth. The first cash flow is desired at age 66 and flows will be required through age 85; a deferred annuity will be purchased at a later date to cover income needs past age 85.

4. Suppose that you also have a client, the Scioscia family, whose breadwinner is 45 years old. The Scioscias are currently positioned with the same 60/30/10 allocation. Their breadwinner is comfortable with keeping the allocation percentages as they currently stand, but he would like to transition the fixed-income portion to create flooring for retirement. If the Scioscias' portfolio currently has a market value of $1,250,000, determine the amount of flooring covering ages 66 through 85 that can be obtained by transitioning the current fixed-income allocation to flooring. *Hint:* Use the table provided in the solution to Problem 3.

5. Suppose that you manage a portfolio for the Griffins. Their breadwinner is 40 years old and is interested in making a rollover distribution from a 401(k) into an IRA and transitioning the entire portfolio for retirement income. Her current $1,000,000 portfolio is allocated for moderately conservative accumulation with a 50/40/10 split between equity, fixed income, and cash. The 401(k) is currently invested in a mix of mutual funds and currently has a market value of $250,000. If the client uses all of the funds in the rollover for flooring, determine

the remaining changes to allocate for a floor at 4 percent of wealth out through age 85.

6. Suppose that your clients, the Stubbs family, want to transition the focus of their portfolio from accumulation to retirement. Suppose further that the Stubbses want to have the retirement income portfolio actively managed as covered in Chapter 9. The accumulation portfolio has had a moderately aggressive posture with an 80 percent weighting to equity. Discuss whether the transition to retirement income requires engaging in transactions to secure the floor.

7. Suppose the Sax family is interested in retirement income but will most likely end up with an underfunded retirement, necessitating tough choices. The client does not want to confront the likely outcome at the present time but instead wants to remain a market participant. Discuss how to transition the client's portfolio for retirement income with the likely outcome of the client needing to annuitize, defer retirement, or reduce circumstances at a later date.

Putting Together the Proposal

Contents

Objectives
Creating proposals to transform from an accumulation focus to a retirement income focus
Making the transformation a natural extension of business

CHAPTER RECAP

This chapter has focused on taking a traditional portfolio construct and positioning a proposal to transform the portfolio into a retirement income portfolio. The adviser needs to make sure that the transformation is backward compatible in the sense that this is an improvement over something that was already good. The natural place to start is to show that the fixed income component of the original portfolio can be transformed to provide a customized solution for the client—one that scales easily for the adviser who needs to serve many clients.

PROBLEMS

The problems for this chapter are qualitative in nature and require that you use your current tools. Therefore, no solutions are provided.

1. Using your firm's style for account statements and balances, determine how you would propose taking a particular client's accumulation portfolio and recasting the portfolio for a retirement income focus.

2. Suppose that the fixed-income allocation of a client's portfolio is dominated by the typical assortment of bond funds of varying duration. Determine how you would propose turning a nonmaturing bond fund into an income floor for your client. Does your approach take the client's tax situation and account structure vis-à-vis taxability?

3. Does your prototypical client seem like the type who wants a level floor (either real or nominal) or a floor taking into account that different stages of retirement might correspond to different lifestyle preferences?

4. Determine whether your client's lifestyle precludes the ability to have capital markets flooring. Determine your proposal to the client for placing a particular type of flooring in their portfolio.

5. Does your client seem prepared for longevity and the other threats to lifestyle that can be insured against (either self-insured or through risk pooling)?

6. Determine whether the precautionary balances in your client's portfolio are sufficient for current needs and whether the precautionary needs will change during retirement.

7. If the current portfolio has a particular weighting of equity, fixed income, and cash, determine the proposed risky portfolio for your client with flooring in place.

8. Determine, with flooring in place, whether your client's risk appetite for the risky portfolio will change. Also determine whether the client's risk appetite with a retirement income portfolio is consistent with the risk appetite for the accumulation approach when no floor was in place.

9. Determine what the pushback points might be; whether it is you or the client that is likely to have pushback points about changing the portfolio.

10. Determine whether your approach will be based on fear or opportunity. Note that insurance often sells on fear; and capital markets products often sell on opportunity.

Market Segmentation

Contents

Objectives

Show how to match clients with product types by market segment
Show segmentation for retirement portfolios
Illustrate segmentation differences between retirement income portfolios
and accumulation portfolios

CHAPTER RECAP

Traditional accumulation portfolios rely on a segmentation designed to differentiate based on the amount of volatility that the client is willing to tolerate. Low-volatility schemes are, by themselves, insufficient for retirement income portfolios. They don't appreciably lower the probability of drowning, but they increase the probability that if drowning occurs, it will be in a shallower pool.

Segmentation for retirement income rests in one dimension on the observable level of client wealth relative to the present value of the client's desired lifestyle. The other dimension for client segmentation in retirement income is the easily observable age of the client. Mapping products into the segmentation structure then becomes a straightforward and natural process.

PROBLEMS

1. Explain the following statement: The traditional approach to client segmentation falling along wealth and risk-tolerance dimensions is a special case of segmentation when there is no consumption floor.

2. Explain how the presence of future consumption needs leads to a segmentation of *some* sort along a lifestyle dimension.

3. Explain why suitability issues do not disappear but the nature of the issues change in life-cycle segmentation versus accumulation segmentation.

4. Gross margins tend to be highest for products that end up in the lowest end (mass market) and the highest end of the wealth spectrum (ultra-high net worth). Discuss the difference in factors that lead to this result.

5. Discuss the implications of habit formation for a client who fits into the underfunded bucket at age 40. In particular, discuss the likelihood of that same client receiving additional wealth and migrating to a different lifestyle bucket at, say age 45.

6. Segmentation based on lifestyle (3 categories) and wealth (4 categories) provided us with a matrix with 12 entries. Having eight categories of age bands (<35, 35–40, 45–50, 50–55, 55–60, 60–65, 65–70, >70) gives us a potentially unmanageable 96 segments. What link between the age groupings simplifies the problem and makes the problem manageable?

Products and Example Portfolios

Contents

Objectives

Provide a categorization of products by type
Provide example portfolios for the commonly served segments
Show examples of how the product choices tend to change by segments

CHAPTER RECAP

This chapter has provided a survey of product groupings that are useful to advisers serving the retirement space. This chapter has also provided a small catalog of examples that advisers can use to frame their approaches to clients in the various segments described in Chapter 12.

PROBLEMS

There are no formal problems associated with this chapter. But here are some issues to think about.

Segmentation based on lifestyle (three categories) and wealth (four categories) in Chapter 12's format provide us with a matrix that consists of 12 entries. Age can be broken down into subgroups, but the main issue is whether clients are preretirement or postretirement.

- Do you have an allocation table that can link clients in different age groups rather than requiring separate portfolio constructs for each age group?
- Do you use combined floor/upside products for the entirety of the portfolio or just as a component?
- Is the client's flooring risk free or sufficiently diversified across issuers?
- Do the portfolios you create have the intention of leading to a capital markets- or insurance-based floor for retirement?
- Does what your clients actually choose to do match your intentions?
- Are you able to compartmentalize the risk of your client portfolios between floor and upside?
- Are your firm's product offerings properly differentiated by client wealth level?
- Are you able to differentiate clients by lifestyle type within a wealth category?
- "Reverse inquiry"—that is, advisers asking product developers for specific products, for which advisers are sure there is demand, is the fastest way to create new products. What are the first three products you would ask for to fill out your client's portfolios?
- Do the portfolios you construct lead to your intended degree of activity in the portfolio and interaction with the client?
- Is the portfolio that you are constructing robust (in a lifestyle sense) to market risk?
- Is the floor of the portfolio that you have constructed robust to the type of systemic risk seen in 2008 or industry risk seen in 2009?

CHAPTER 14

Preparing Your Client for a Retirement Income Portfolio

Contents

Know Your Resources
Lifestyle and Life Cycle
Risks to Your Retirement Lifestyle
Lifestyle and Flooring Types
What the Adviser Needs from the Client

Objectives

Provide information that can be supplied directly to clients to help them understand the process of creating a retirement income portfolio
Help clients understand what information you need from them
Help clients understand what you will be doing for them

CHAPTER RECAP

Creating the right retirement portfolio for you is a job that requires you to provide your adviser with some information. You know your resources and your plans and the more completely you can convey the information to your adviser, the better the outcome that you can expect. Your adviser will need to know a few things from you:

- About when you plan to retire
- How you want to be able to live
- Your willingness to save today for your goals tomorrow
- What you want to leave for future generations
- What the important risks are for you
- Your resources for meeting your goals

PROBLEMS

There are no formal problems associated with this chapter. However, the following table lists the actions that require ownership of responsibility:

	Client's Responsibility	Adviser's Responsibility
Balance Sheet		
Assets:		
Financial wealth		
Human capital		
Social capital		
Liabilities:		
Mortgage		
Fixed debts		
Income Statement		
Earnings		
Other income		
Lifestyle necessities		
Lifestyle enhancers		
Loop Back to Balance Sheet		
PV of lifestyle necessities		
Capacity for Bequest		
Transition		
Allocation of current assets		
Plan of accumulation for retirement		
Management of portfolio		
Distribution of funds		

CHAPTER 15

Salvage Operations, Mistakes, and Fallacies

Contents

Objectives

Illuminate common mistakes and debunk some myths about long-run performance and long-run risk

Developing techniques and plans for helping clients recover from financial disaster

CHAPTER RECAP

In the field of retail finance, there are many solutions that are offered for treating "sick" portfolios. Many of these proposed solutions are nothing more than the financial equivalent of folk remedies that generally offer no improvement in prospects and may make things worse. In the wake of the Panic of '08, where the credibility of financial advice is being questioned more than ever, it is time to offer clients reliability. Therefore, this chapter debunks some of the myths around long-run risk. The long run is risky. Risk increases with the time horizon. There is a vast distinction to be made between where the market tells us that the odds are in our favor and where we only have a hope that the odds are in our favor.

We also delve into practical steps for making the best of a bad situation. Lives have been ruined by a business model that for 25 years was tolerant of mistaken beliefs, and bad advice. The reputation and viability of the retail industry has not been more in doubt since the 1930s. Many of you who have read this far are worried about your future. Instead of focusing on the extremity of the related challenges faced by clients and the financial services industry, this book has been about creating a business model that is more beneficial for clients and advisers alike. I hope it is beneficial to you and your clients.

Trillions of dollars in client assets were vaporized last year. For many whose wealth declined, the recriminations are nearing their end and the planning for gaining back lost ground is beginning. Advisers need a plan to help clients to both restore their portfolios and restore trust in their advisers.

PROBLEMS

We began the workbook with a preview of notation and a debunking of the fallacy that stocks are less risky in the long run. What we showed was that the fallacy was predicated on looking at average returns rather than cumulative returns. Cumulative returns constitute a sum of random variables rather than an average.

Still the fallacy persists in other forms. Another way that this fallacy represents itself is with the notion that with an expected return greater than the risk-free rate, waiting long enough will always pay off. However, insurance for the portfolio reflects the cost of nullifying the risk in the portfolio; the cost of nullifying the risk is a fairly constant proportion of the value, no matter how long the horizon and no matter whether the mean or volatility is mean reverting, in fact, no matter what the distribution of returns looks like.

Use the following information to answer questions 1–3:

Suppose that the risk-free rate is constant at 3 percent, the cost of borrowing shares to take a short position is 50 basis points per year (0.5 percent). The stock of ABC has a current market value of $100 per share and pays a quarterly dividend of $0.60. Suppose that the funds from a short position are deposited in a risk-free account out of which borrow costs and dividends are to be paid. Dividends are paid at the end of the quarter.

1. Suppose 100 shares are shorted and the proceeds are placed in a risk-free account. Find the amount in the account if the short is maintained for 1, 3, 5, 10, and 25 years,

2. Suppose that ABC stock has an expected return of 20 percent and a volatility of 0 percent. Determine the impact of knowing the expected return and volatility on the proceeds of selling ABC short.

3. Suppose that your client, the Iguchi family, wants to engage in a contract to insure the portfolio and lock in a guaranteed price, today, on ABC 15 years from today. Determine the most that the counterparty, unwilling to take uncompensated risks, would offer for the shares of ABC 15 years from today. Discuss why the answer is an upper bound.

Use the following information for Problems 4–7:
A risky portfolio is being compared to a risk-free portfolio. If the risk-free rate is a continuously compounded rate of 3 percent, and the mean and variance of the risky portfolio are 8 percent and 15 percent respectively, assume that the lognormal distribution applies to the risky portfolio.

$$\text{Ln}(V_T) - \text{Ln}(V_0) = \left(r - \frac{\sigma^2}{2} \right) \times T + \sigma Z \sqrt{T}$$

$$\Rightarrow V_T = V_0 e^{\left(r - \frac{\sigma^2}{2} \right) T + \sigma Z \sqrt{T}}$$

with

$$\text{Expected}[V_T] = V_0 \times e^{rT}$$

$$\sigma_{V_T} = V_0 \sqrt{e^{2rT} \left(e^{T\sigma^2} - 1 \right)}$$

A value of $Z = -1.645$ provides the bound for the lower 5 percent of this probability distribution, that is, values more negative than -1.645 occur less than 5 percent of the time, and a value of below $Z = -.84$ occurs 20 percent of the time.

4. Find the expected value of the Dye family's portfolio. They currently have a $1,000,000 portfolio invested in the risk-free asset. The Dyes want to know what will be in the portfolio at the end of 10 years.

5. Find the expected value of the Podsednik family's portfolio. They currently have a $1,000,000 portfolio that is completely invested in the risky portfolio. The Podsedniks want to know what the expected value of their portfolio will be at the end of 10 years.

6. The Uribe family is cautious. They want to know the value of their $1,000,000 portfolio invested in the risky portfolio at the end of 10 years assuming a Z value of -1.645.

7. Find the Z value for the risky portfolio ending up with the same value of the risky portfolio after 10 years.

8. (Advanced) Find the general rule for finding the Z value such that the value of the risky portfolio equals the value of the risk-free portfolio after T years. (Recognize the result?)

9. Suppose that the Rowand family is an accumulation client. The Rowands have suffered a 30 percent loss on their portfolio in the last year. If the PV of their consumption needs is 90 percent of the remaining portfolio, discuss the triage options for this client.

10. Suppose that the risk-free rate is 3 percent. The Garcia family is a client who has a PV of consumption needs of $1,000,000. The client breadwinner expects to retire in one year. The current portfolio value is $1,200,000. Suppose that there is a risky portfolio available that has an expected return of 10 percent and a standard deviation of 14 percent. Find the Z value for this client's portfolio missing the consumption hurdle on the retirement date. (Before solving this problem ask yourself to guess on the odds of failure.)

11. Suppose that the Everetts are your new clients. The Everetts have fully and irrevocably retired and must make the best of their portfolio. At its peak, their portfolio was worth $3,000,000. The Everetts enjoy taking risks, but they have come to you because they feel that their lifestyle is now in danger. Having fallen from its peak, their portfolio is now only worth $2,000,000. Having suffered a substantial loss, they have come to you to restructure their portfolio and suggest a path to recovery. You have calculated the present value of their lifestyle needs, inclusive of all debt obligations, longevity needs, and precautionary needs. Satisfying their needs will require $1,750,000 of their financial capital. Discuss the options available to the Everetts to dig out of the hole in which they have found themselves.

Problems 12–18 cover some of the topics in the book and also help to explain the plunge in consumption that occurred in the fall of 2008. We'll start with the simplest possible framework.

For an individual with constant relative risk aversion, no impatience, and no minimum consumption lifestyle, it is shown in the appendix that the optimal rate for consuming out of wealth depends only on the number of years remaining, that is,

$$f_t^{Pct} = \frac{1}{T - t + 1},$$

where T is the (known) final date and t is today.

12. Suppose that retirement is at age 65 and death by age 105 is a certainty. Use the preceding formula to find the percentage of wealth that would be consumed by a client at age 34, 54, and age 64.

Use the following information for Problems 13–17:

Suppose that it is now January 1. A 34-year-old client earns $100,000 per year, paid annually on the date of birth (December 31). Retirement commences the day after turning 65. Our client's other assets include a $200,000 portfolio and a $1,000,000 house with a mortgage of $800,000. Our client discounts future earnings at 4 percent.

13. Create this client's economic balance sheet and amount of this year's consumption.
14. Suppose that, other things constant, the client suffers a 40 percent decline in portfolio value. Find the new level of consumption.
15. Using the original information, suppose that our client gets laid off for a full year, but expectations are for a full recovery after that.
16. Using the original information, find the new level of consumption if the client becomes fearful of maintaining future employment and begins discounting future earnings at 5 percent.
17. Using the original information, suppose that housing prices fall by 40 percent. Find the new level of consumption.
18. Discuss which factors, of those given in Problems 13–17, led to the largest percentage drops in consumption.

Solutions

CHAPTER 1

Portfolio Focus and Stage of Life

1. The simple average return $\bar{x}$ is generally written in the following form:

$$\bar{x} = \frac{\sum_{i=1}^{n} x_i}{n}$$
$$= x_1 + x_2 + \cdots + x_n$$

Using our sample of data, the simple average can be found by taking the sum of returns and dividing by $n = 20$:

$$\bar{x} = \frac{140\%}{20} = 7\%$$

2. The geometric average return $\bar{g}$ is generally written in the following form:

$$\bar{g} = \left(\prod_{i=1}^{n} (1 + x_i) \right)^{1/n} - 1$$
$$= ((1 + x_1)(1 + x_2) \cdots (1 + x_n))^{1/n} - 1$$

Using our sample of data, the geometric average can be found by taking the product of gross returns and dividing by $n = 20$:

$$\bar{g} = (291\%)^{1/20} - 1 = 5.49\%$$

3. The portfolio of the Scott family would grow to $6,757,569 over the 20-year period. During pure accumulation, the Scott family is well served by sticking to their plan for saving money. As we will see in the table, this will give us yet another example of a plan that works well

for pure accumulation but is disastrous during withdrawal: The properties that provide the benefits during accumulation are drawbacks in withdrawal.

Period	Beginning of Period Portfolio Value	Deposit	Return	End of Period Portfolio
1	$1,000,000	$50,000	10%	$1,155,000
2	$1,155,000	$50,000	−10%	$1,084,500
3	$1,084,500	$50,000	−10%	$1,021,050
4	$1,021,050	$50,000	10%	$1,178,155
5	$1,178,155	$50,000	−10%	$1,105,340
6	$1,105,340	$50,000	−10%	$1,039,806
7	$1,039,806	$50,000	−10%	$980,825
8	$980,825	$50,000	−10%	$927,742
9	$927,742	$50,000	−10%	$879,968
10	$879,968	$50,000	−10%	$836,971
11	$836,971	$50,000	−10%	$798,274
12	$798,274	$50,000	−10%	$763,447
13	$763,447	$50,000	10%	$894,792
14	$894,792	$50,000	30%	$1,228,229
15	$1,228,229	$50,000	30%	$1,661,698
16	$1,661,698	$50,000	30%	$2,225,207
17	$2,225,207	$50,000	30%	$2,957,769
18	$2,957,769	$50,000	30%	$3,910,100
19	$3,910,100	$50,000	30%	$5,148,130
20	$5,148,130	$50,000	30%	$6,757,569

4. The portfolio of the Scott family started with a value of $1,000,000 and grew to $6,757,569 over the 20-year period. The geometric average growth rate can be found by taking

$$
\begin{aligned}
\text{Geometric growth rate} &= \left(\frac{\text{Final value}}{\text{Initial value}} \right)^{1/\text{Number of periods}} - 1 \\
&= \left(\frac{\$6,757,969}{\$1,000,000} \right)^{1/20} - 1 \\
&= 10.02\%
\end{aligned}
$$

5. The funds that the Andrews family possesses as they begin their withdrawal plan are sufficient to last for 20 years. The following table shows that at the end of the 20-year period, the Andrews family still has $246,782 in remaining funds. Even putting the funds in a mattress

earning 0% would have worked. This problem is meant to emphasize the existence of a safe alternative for a client whose retirement is fully funded.

Period	Beginning of Period Portfolio Value	Withdrawal	Return	End of Period Portfolio
1	$1,000,000	$50,000	2%	$969,000
2	$969,000	$50,000	2%	$937,380
3	$937,380	$50,000	2%	$905,128
4	$905,128	$50,000	2%	$872,230
5	$872,230	$50,000	2%	$838,675
6	$838,675	$50,000	2%	$804,448
7	$804,448	$50,000	2%	$769,537
8	$769,537	$50,000	2%	$733,928
9	$733,928	$50,000	2%	$697,607
10	$697,607	$50,000	2%	$660,559
11	$660,559	$50,000	2%	$622,770
12	$622,770	$50,000	2%	$584,225
13	$584,225	$50,000	2%	$544,910
14	$544,910	$50,000	2%	$504,808
15	$504,808	$50,000	2%	$463,904
16	$463,904	$50,000	2%	$422,182
17	$422,182	$50,000	2%	$379,626
18	$379,626	$50,000	2%	$336,218
19	$336,218	$50,000	2%	$291,943
20	$291,943	$50,000	2%	$246,782

6. The Petrocelli family is retiring and the family wants to draw down the $1,000,000 portfolio by $50,000 per year. As the following table demonstrates, their funds will not last for 20 years. In fact, they come up short after only 13 years.

Period	Beginning of Period Portfolio Value	Return	Gross Portfolio at End of Period	Withdrawal	End of Period Portfolio
1	$1,000,000	10%	$1,100,000	$50,000	$1,050,000
2	$1,050,000	−10%	$945,000	$50,000	$895,000
3	$895,000	−10%	$805,500	$50,000	$755,500
4	$755,500	10%	$831,050	$50,000	$781,050
5	$781,050	−10%	$702,945	$50,000	$652,945
6	$652,945	−10%	$587,651	$50,000	$537,651

(*Continued*)

Period	Beginning of Period Portfolio Value	Return	Gross Portfolio at End of Period	Withdrawal	End of Period Portfolio
7	$537,651	−10%	$483,885	$50,000	$433,885
8	$433,885	−10%	$390,497	$50,000	$340,497
9	$340,497	−10%	$306,447	$50,000	$256,447
10	$256,447	−10%	$230,802	$50,000	$180,802
11	$180,802	−10%	$162,722	$50,000	$112,722
12	$112,722	−10%	$101,450	$50,000	$51,450
13	$51,450	10%	$56,595	$50,000	$6,595
14	$6,595	30%	$8,574	$8,574	$—
15	$—	30%	$—	$—	$—
16	$—	30%	$—	$—	$—
17	$—	30%	$—	$—	$—
18	$—	30%	$—	$—	$—
19	$—	30%	$—	$—	$—
20	$—	30%	$—	$—	$—

7. The Foys use their perfect foresight and know the return stream given at the start of this section will occur. To the nearest $250, find the maximum annual withdrawal that the Foys can take from the account that will be guaranteed to last for 20 years. Using trial and error, we can see that the most that they can take from the portfolio each year and have the portfolio last for the full 20 years is $38,750

Period	Beginning of Period Portfolio Value	Return	Gross Portfolio at End of Period	Withdrawal	End of Period Portfolio
1	$1,000,000	10%	$1,100,000	$38,750	$1,061,250
2	$1,061,250	−10%	$955,125	$38,750	$916,375
3	$916,375	−10%	$824,738	$38,750	$785,988
4	$785,988	10%	$864,586	$38,750	$825,836
5	$825,836	−10%	$743,253	$38,750	$704,503
6	$704,503	−10%	$634,052	$38,750	$595,302
7	$595,302	−10%	$535,772	$38,750	$497,022
8	$497,022	−10%	$447,320	$38,750	$408,570
9	$408,570	−10%	$367,713	$38,750	$328,963

Period	Beginning of Period Portfolio Value	Return	Gross Portfolio at End of Period	Withdrawal	End of Period Portfolio
10	$328,963	−10%	$296,067	$38,750	$257,317
11	$257,317	−10%	$231,585	$38,750	$192,835
12	$192,835	−10%	$173,551	$38,750	$134,801
13	$134,801	10%	$148,282	$38,750	$109,532
14	$109,532	30%	$142,391	$38,750	$103,641
15	$103,641	30%	$134,733	$38,750	$95,983
16	$95,983	30%	$124,778	$38,750	$86,028
17	$86,028	30%	$111,837	$38,750	$73,087
18	$73,087	30%	$95,013	$38,750	$56,263
19	$56,263	30%	$73,142	$38,750	$34,392
20	$34,392	30%	$44,710	$38,750	$5,960

8. The Howard family is more concerned with making sure that the money lasts rather than maintaining a specific lifestyle. They adjust their retirement lifestyle each year to make sure that the money lasts for 20 years, drawing down at the beginning of each year by 1/the remaining number of years, that is, 1/20, 1/19, 1/18, ..., 1/2, 1.

Period	Beginning of Period Portfolio Value	Withdrawal	Return	End of Period Portfolio
1	$1,000,000	$50,000	10%	$1,045,000
2	$1,045,000	$55,000	−10%	$891,000
3	$891,000	$49,500	−10%	$757,350
4	$757,350	$44,550	10%	$784,080
5	$784,080	$49,005	−10%	$661,568
6	$661,568	$44,105	−10%	$555,717
7	$555,717	$39,694	−10%	$464,420
8	$464,420	$35,725	−10%	$385,826
9	$385,826	$32,152	−10%	$318,307
10	$318,307	$28,937	−10%	$260,433
11	$260,433	$26,043	−10%	$210,950
12	$210,950	$23,439	−10%	$168,760
13	$168,760	$21,095	10%	$162,432
14	$162,432	$23,205	30%	$180,995

(*Continued*)

Period	Beginning of Period Portfolio Value	Withdrawal	Return	End of Period Portfolio
15	$180,995	$30,166	30%	$196,078
16	$196,078	$39,216	30%	$203,922
17	$203,922	$50,980	30%	$198,824
18	$198,824	$66,275	30%	$172,314
19	$172,314	$86,157	30%	$112,004
20	$112,004	$112,004	30%	$—

Although the Howards achieve their goal of making the money last, their lifestyle incurs substantial variability. Due to the pattern of returns in this example, their best years are toward the end of their retirement and the pattern incorporates some lean years where it could be assumed that they would prefer a more active lifestyle.

9. Using a flat 3 percent yield curve for Treasury securities, find the present value of a 20-year annuity that pays $50,000 at the beginning of each period.

Period	Payment	PV Formula	PV Factor	Present Value
1	$50,000	PV(3%,0,$50,000)	1.000	$50,000
2	$50,000	PV(3%,1,$50000)	0.971	$48,544
3	$50,000	PV(3%,2,$50,000)	0.943	$47,130
4	$50,000	PV(3%,3,$50,000)	0.915	$45,757
5	$50,000	PV(3%,4,$50000)	0.888	$44,424
6	$50,000	PV(3%,5,$50,000)	0.863	$43,130
7	$50,000	PV(3%,6,$50,000)	0.837	$41,874
8	$50,000	PV(3%,7,$50000)	0.813	$40,655
9	$50,000	PV(3%,8,$50,000)	0.789	$39,470
10	$50,000	PV(3%,9,$50,000)	0.766	$38,321
11	$50,000	PV(3%,10,$50000)	0.744	$37,205
12	$50,000	PV(3%,11,$50,000)	0.722	$36,121
13	$50,000	PV(3%,12,$50,000)	0.701	$35,069
14	$50,000	PV(3%,13,$50000)	0.681	$34,048
15	$50,000	PV(3%,14,$50,000)	0.661	$33,056
16	$50,000	PV(3%,15,$50,000)	0.642	$32,093
17	$50,000	PV(3%,16,$50000)	0.623	$31,158
18	$50,000	PV(3%,17,$50,000)	0.605	$30,251
19	$50,000	PV(3%,18,$50,000)	0.587	$29,370
20	$50,000	PV(3%,19,$50000)	0.570	$28,514
		Total	15.324	$766,190

10. The Smiths' annuity costs $766,190 (see answer to Problem 9). The remainder is drawn down as in Problem 8. We see that every period provides income above the $50,000 lifestyle threshold that they want to maintain, at least for a fixed window of 20 years.

Period	Beginning of Period Portfolio Value	Withdrawal	Return	End of Period Portfolio	Income
1	$233,810	$11,691	10%	$244,331	$61,691
2	$244,331	$12,860	−10%	$208,325	$62,860
3	$208,325	$11,574	−10%	$177,076	$61,574
4	$177,076	$10,416	10%	$183,326	$60,416
5	$183,326	$11,458	−10%	$154,681	$61,458
6	$154,681	$10,312	−10%	$129,932	$60,312
7	$129,932	$9,281	−10%	$108,586	$59,281
8	$108,586	$8,353	−10%	$90,210	$58,353
9	$90,210	$7,518	−10%	$74,423	$57,518
10	$74,423	$6,766	−10%	$60,892	$56,766
11	$60,892	$6,089	−10%	$49,322	$56,089
12	$49,322	$5,480	−10%	$39,458	$55,480
13	$39,458	$4,932	10%	$37,978	$54,932
14	$37,978	$5,425	30%	$42,319	$55,425
15	$42,319	$7,053	30%	$45,845	$57,053
16	$45,845	$9,169	30%	$47,679	$59,169
17	$47,679	$11,920	30%	$46,487	$61,920
18	$46,487	$15,496	30%	$40,289	$65,496
19	$40,289	$20,144	30%	$26,188	$70,144
20	$26,188	$26,188	30%	$—	$76,188

Research analysts have a feeling that the next period will bring returns of 40 percent. Suppose that they are correct, but that the remaining returns for periods 2 through 20 are as before.

11. Find the simple sample average return for the 20-year period assuming a 40% return in period 1:

$$\bar{x} = \frac{\sum_{i=1}^{n} x_i}{n}$$
$$= x_1 + x_2 + \cdots + x_n$$
$$= \frac{170\%}{20} = 8.5\%$$

12. Find the geometric average return for the 20-year period assuming a 40% return in period 1:

$$\bar{g} = \left(\prod_{i=1}^{n} (1 + x_i) \right)^{1/n} - 1$$
$$= ((1 + x_1)(1 + x_2) \cdots (1 + x_n))^{1/n} - 1$$
$$= (371\%)^{1/20} - 1 = 6.77\%$$

13. The Tartabulls payout profile will be as in the following table:

Period	Beginning of Period Portfolio Value	Withdrawal	Return	End of Period Portfolio
1	$1,000,000	$50,000	40%	$1,330,000
2	$1,330,000	$50,000	-10%	$1,152,000
3	$1,152,000	$50,000	-10%	$991,800
4	$991,800	$50,000	10%	$1,035,980
5	$1,035,980	$50,000	-10%	$887,382
6	$887,382	$50,000	-10%	$753,644
7	$753,644	$50,000	-10%	$633,279
8	$633,279	$50,000	-10%	$524,951
9	$524,951	$50,000	-10%	$427,456
10	$427,456	$50,000	-10%	$339,711
11	$339,711	$50,000	-10%	$260,740
12	$260,740	$50,000	-10%	$189,666
13	$189,666	$50,000	10%	$153,632
14	$153,632	$50,000	30%	$134,722
15	$134,722	$50,000	30%	$110,138
16	$110,138	$50,000	30%	$78,180
17	$78,180	$50,000	30%	$36,634
18	$36,634	$36,634	30%	$—
19	$—	$—	30%	$—
20	$—	$—	30%	$—

As we can see, the Tartabulls are unable to fund their lifestyle beyond year 17.

14. Even with the withdrawals made at the end of the year, and average returns greater than 5% (5% × $1,000,000 = $50,000) the volatility and pattern of returns make the lifestyle unsustainable.

Period	Beginning of Period Portfolio Value	Return	Gross Portfolio at End of Period	Withdrawal	End of Period Portfolio
1	$1,000,000	40%	$1,400,000	$50,000	$1,350,000
2	$1,350,000	–10%	$1,215,000	$50,000	$1,165,000
3	$1,165,000	–10%	$1,048,500	$50,000	$998,500
4	$998,500	10%	$1,098,350	$50,000	$1,048,350
5	$1,048,350	–10%	$943,515	$50,000	$893,515
6	$893,515	–10%	$804,164	$50,000	$754,164
7	$754,164	–10%	$678,747	$50,000	$628,747
8	$628,747	–10%	$565,872	$50,000	$515,872
9	$515,872	–10%	$464,285	$50,000	$414,285
10	$414,285	–10%	$372,857	$50,000	$322,857
11	$322,857	–10%	$290,571	$50,000	$240,571
12	$240,571	–10%	$216,514	$50,000	$166,514
13	$166,514	10%	$183,165	$50,000	$133,165
14	$133,165	30%	$173,115	$50,000	$123,115
15	$123,115	30%	$160,049	$50,000	$110,049
16	$110,049	30%	$143,064	$50,000	$93,064
17	$93,064	30%	$120,983	$50,000	$70,983
18	$70,983	30%	$92,278	$50,000	$42,278
19	$42,278	30%	$54,962	$50,000	$4,962
20	$4,962	30%	$6,451	$6,451	$—

15. The Tiants live on $50,000 per year, received at the beginning of the year. Their adviser created a $50,000 income stream for them using treasury securities, placing the unallocated funds in a risky account with the returns stream as in Problems 1–9. At the end of the 20-year period, find how much they will have leftover to fund potential longevity.

From Problem 9, we know the cost of the annuity is $766,190. This leaves $233,810 for deposit into the risky fund. Following the return pattern provided, the geometric yield of 5.49 percent indicates that the fund will end with roughly $680,900. We can also see this in tabular form.

Period	Beginning of Period Portfolio Value	Return	End of Period Portfolio
1	$233,810	10%	$257,191
2	$257,191	–10%	$231,472
3	$231,472	–10%	$208,325

(*Continued*)

Period	Beginning of Period Portfolio Value	Return	End of Period Portfolio
4	$208,325	10%	$229,157
5	$229,157	−10%	$206,242
6	$206,242	−10%	$185,617
7	$185,617	−10%	$167,056
8	$167,056	−10%	$150,350
9	$150,350	−10%	$135,315
10	$135,315	−10%	$121,784
11	$121,784	−10%	$109,605
12	$109,605	−10%	$98,645
13	$98,645	10%	$108,509
14	$108,509	30%	$141,062
15	$141,062	30%	$183,380
16	$183,380	30%	$238,395
17	$238,395	30%	$309,913
18	$309,913	30%	$402,887
19	$402,887	30%	$523,753
20	$523,753	30%	$680,879

In this case, the client ends up with enough to fund several more years of the desired lifestyle. However, with extreme longevity, the client could still run out of assets before running out of time.

16. If the funds are invested in a riskless account, yielding 3 percent per year, then the portfolio will grow to $1,000,000 \times 1.03^{20} = \$1,806,111$. If, on the other hand, the risky portfolio has a 90 percent probability of providing the results of the following formula:

$$\text{Ln}(V_T) - \text{Ln}(V_0) = \left(r - \frac{\sigma^2}{2}\right) \times T + \sigma Z\sqrt{T}$$

$$\Rightarrow V_T = V_0 e^{\left(r - \frac{\sigma^2}{2}\right)T + \sigma Z\sqrt{T}}$$

$$= \$1,000,000 e^{\left(.07 - \frac{0.12^2}{2}\right)20 + Z0.12\sqrt{20}}$$

For $Z = -1.645$, $V_T = \$1,452,375$

For $Z = 1.645$, $V_T = \$8,489,241$

17. Using the formula provided, the expected value and standard deviation of the portfolio in 16 years will be

$$\text{Expected}[V_{16}] = \$1,000,000 \times e^{16 \times 8\%} = \$3,596,640$$

$$\sigma_{V_{16}} = \sqrt{\$1,000,000^2 \times e^{2 \times 16 \times 8\%}\left(e^{16 \times 0.15^2} - 1\right)} = \$2,367,587$$

Note that normality and symmetry of portfolio *returns* means that the distribution of portfolio *values* is asymmetric.

18. A bullet payment in 16 years will be worth $(1.04)^{16} = 1.872981$ times the starting value. Starting with a million dollars the Adairs are certain to end up with $\$1,872,981$.

19. For the Joneses to end up at or worse off than the Adairs would imply the following:

$$\$1,872,981 \geq \$1,000,000 \times e^{\left(\left(.08 - \frac{.2^2}{2}\right)16 - z \times .2 \times \sqrt{16}\right)}$$

$$\Rightarrow Ln(1.872981) \geq \left(\left(.08 - \frac{.2^2}{2}\right)16 - z \times .2 \times \sqrt{16}\right) = .96 - z \times .8$$

$$\Rightarrow \left(\frac{Ln(1.872981)}{.8}\right) - 1.2 = -0.41559 \geq z$$

The probability of this event under the normal distribution is 34%.

CHAPTER 2

The Top-Down View

A Short Primer on Economic Models of Retirement Income

1. Find the expected return, variance, and standard deviation for Portfolio 1.

For a discrete probability distribution, the mean, variance, and standard deviation are given with the more general formulas for discrete distributions:

$$\text{Mean} = \sum_{i=1}^{N} \text{Probability}_i \times \text{Outcome}_i$$
$$= .7 \times .2 + .3 \times -.2 = 8\%$$

$$\text{Variance} = \sum_{i=1}^{N} \text{probability}_i \times (\text{Outcome}_i - \text{Mean})^2$$
$$= .7 \times (.20 - .08)^2 + .3 \times (-.20 - .08)^2 = .0336$$

$$\text{Standard deviation} = \sqrt{\text{Variance}}$$
$$= \sqrt{0.0336} = 18.33\%$$

2. Find the expected return, variance, and standard deviation for Portfolio 2.

$$\text{Mean} = \sum_{i=1}^{N} \text{Probability}_i \times \text{Outcome}_i$$
$$= .1 \times .7 + .9 \times 0 = 7\%$$

$$\text{Variance} = \sum_{i=1}^{N} \text{Probability}_i \times (\text{Outcome}_i - \text{Mean})^2$$
$$= .1 \times (.70 - .07)^2 + .9 \times (0 - .07)^2 = .0441$$

$$\text{Standard deviation} = \sqrt{\text{Variance}}$$
$$= \sqrt{0.0441} = 21.00\%$$

3. Determine which portfolio will be preferred by a mean/variance investor.

	Portfolio 1	Portfolio 2
Mean	8%	7%
Variance	0.0336	0.0441
Standard Deviation	18.33%	21.00%

Portfolio 1 has both a higher mean and a lower variance than Portfolio 2. Portfolio 1 offers both first and second order stochastic dominance. A mean/variance investor will prefer Portfolio 1 as the higher return, lower risk portfolio.

4. For an investor with an initial investment of $100 and utility function is given by $U = \text{Expected(Final wealth)} - \dfrac{\text{Variance(Final wealth)}}{100}$, Portfolio 1 will provide the higher expected utility.

For Portfolio 1:

$$U_{P1} = \sum_{i=1}^{n} \text{Probability} \times U(\text{Outcome}_i)$$

$$= 100 \times 1.08 - \frac{100^2 \times .0336}{100}$$

$$= 108 - 3.36 = 104.64$$

For Portfolio 2:

$$U_{P2} = \sum_{i=1}^{n} \text{Probability} \times U(\text{Outcome}_i)$$

$$= 100 \times 1.07 - \frac{100^2 \times .0441}{100} = 102.59$$

5. In contrast, this investor would not even consider Portfolio 1 since it has an outcome that violates the minimum consumption need of $85. With this utility function and its floor, Portfolio 2 becomes the preferred portfolio.

6. For an investor with an initial investment of $100 and utility function is given by $U = \sqrt{\text{Final wealth}}$, Portfolio 1 will provide the higher expected utility.

For Portfolio 1:

$$U_{P1} = \sum_{i=1}^{n} \text{Probability} \times U(\text{Outcome}_i)$$

$$= .7 \times \sqrt{120} + .3 \times \sqrt{80} = 10.3514$$

For Portfolio 2:

$$U_{P2} = \sum_{i=1}^{n} \text{Probability} \times U(\text{Outcome}_i)$$
$$= .1 \times \sqrt{170} + .9 \times \sqrt{100} = 10.3038$$

7. In contrast, assume that the investor's initially investment is $100 and the investor's utility function is now given by $U = \sqrt{\text{Final wealth} - 80}$. Find the preferred portfolio.

For Portfolio 1:

$$U_{P1} = \sum_{i=1}^{n} \text{Probability} \times U(\text{Outcome}_i)$$
$$= .7 \times \sqrt{120 - 80} + .3 \times \sqrt{80 - 80} = 4.4272$$

For Portfolio 2:

$$U_{P2} = \sum_{i=1}^{n} \text{Probability} \times U(\text{Outcome}_i)$$
$$= .1 \times \sqrt{170 - 80} + .9 \times \sqrt{100 - 80} = 4.9736$$

With this utility function, Portfolio 2 becomes the preferred portfolio.

8. As soon as a consumption floor is included, the outcomes that exceed the floor become much more important for creating satisfaction. Even though Portfolio 1 has both lower variance and higher expected return than Portfolio 2, Portfolio 2 has less lifestyle risk and becomes preferred.

As an aside: It is interesting to note that if the floor had been set above 80, then the investor would not even be willing to consider Portfolio 1. The adviser does not observe the client's utility function, but does observe what sells. The import of the above statements is that to the adviser who only observes behavior and not the underlying motivation, the client may seem to be acting suboptimally by refusing a portfolio that dominates in mean and variance. Some may even be tempted to call the client irrational. In fact, the client isn't acting suboptimally; it is that a small change in objective can lead to a large change in optimal solutions.

Some of the tension between practitioners and academics may derive from practitioners observing that so-called "optimal" portfolios don't sell very well. Clients may be acting perfectly rationally, but it appears irrational because they aren't acting in the way that the simple model would predict.

What is really happening is that optimization is always with respect to a particular objective. If the objective is misstated then the optimal solution will be misstated: Use the wrong model, get the wrong answer. When used properly, models give us impressions of reality, but not clear depictions. Models are just toys that need to be taken with a dose of healthy skepticism. The other side of the coin is also true: just because the simple model isn't adequate to explain behavior doesn't mean that we need to throw out the entire framework of utility.

9. Our client has a flooring need of $50,000 over the next 40 years. The treasury yield curve is flat at 4 percent so the flooring can be calculated as an ordinary 40 period annuity with a discount rate of 4 percent.

Answer = $989,638.69.

The following information is used in Problems 10–14:
Suppose that the client has $1,000,000 in assets and is willing to take diversified credit risk in creating an income floor. Suppose further that there are two closed-end corporate bond funds that will make level payments over some interval.

	Fund A	Fund B
Coverage	20 years	40 years
Level	1$/yr	1$/yr
Mkt Price	$11.47	$14.82

The funds consist of A- and AA-rated bonds and each share will provide a level stream of $1 per year over the coverage period.

In addition, assume that there are 2 diversified risky funds having the following properties:

	Risky Fund C	Risky Fund D
Mean Return	8%	14%
Standard Deviation	16%	24%

10. Find the cost of creating both 20-year and 40-year level flooring at $50,000 for this client, and the amount of the remainder funds that can be placed in the risky funds in each of the cases.

The 20-year flooring costs $11.47 × $50,000 = $573,500

The 40-year flooring costs $14.82 × $50,000 = $741,000

Opting for 20 years of flooring, the client would have $426,500 left over for investment in risky assets. If the client chooses 40 years of flooring then there will be $259,000 left over for investment in risky assets.

11. Find the yield to maturity on each of the flooring funds using trial and error in a spreadsheet:

Period	PV Factors 20 Year	PV Factors 40 Year
1	0.94	0.94
2	0.89	0.89
3	0.84	0.84
4	0.79	0.79
5	0.75	0.74
6	0.70	0.70
7	0.67	0.66
8	0.63	0.62
9	0.59	0.59
10	0.56	0.55
11	0.53	0.52
12	0.50	0.49
13	0.47	0.46
14	0.44	0.44
15	0.42	0.41
16	0.39	0.39
17	0.37	0.36
18	0.35	0.34
19	0.33	0.32
20	0.31	0.30
21		0.29
22		0.27
23		0.25
24		0.24
25		0.23
26		0.21
27		0.20
28		0.19
29		0.18
30		0.17
31		0.16
32		0.15
33		0.14

(*Continued*)

Period	PV Factors 20 Year	PV Factors 40 Year
34		0.13
35		0.12
36		0.12
37		0.11
38		0.10
39		0.10
40		0.09
Sum	11.47	14.81

20-year YTM = 6 percent; 40-year YTM = 6.125 percent.

12. The initial portfolio value is $1,000,000.

For the 20-year option, flooring costs $11.47 × $50,000 = $573,500 making the portfolio weights: 0.5735 flooring; 0.4265 risky.

For the 40-year option, flooring costs $14.82 × $50,000 = $741,000 making the portfolio weights: 0.741 flooring; 0.259 risky.

13. For the 20-year portfolio:

$$E[r] = 0.5735 \times .06 + .4625 \times .08 = 6.853\%$$

$$\sigma = \sqrt{0.5735 \times .01^2 + 0.4625 \times .16^2} = \sqrt{.010976} = 10.4765\%$$

14. For the 40-year portfolio:

$$E[r] = 0.741 \times .06125 + 0.259 \times .14 = 8.1646\%$$

$$\sigma = \sqrt{0.741 \times .015^2 + 0.259 \times .24^2} = \sqrt{.015185} = 12.2822\%$$

The Value of Insurance and Monetizing Mortality

15. Once flooring is secured, the client may be willing to take more risk than in a portfolio that leaves lifestyle unsecured.

16. The rate that makes the individual indifferent is given by the following:

$$U = .7 \times 1.2^{.5} + .3 \times .8^{.5} = (1+x)^{.5}$$
$$= 1.03514$$
$$\Rightarrow x = (1.03514)^2 - 1 = 7.1514\%$$

The importance is that at this rate, the client will prefer to avoid risk; any risk-free alternative offering a higher yield will be preferred.

17. With the client's utility function given by $U = \sqrt{\text{Final wealth}}$ (note that final consumption = final wealth), the client will prefer placing $95,000 in the risky asset given in Problem 15.

With the annuity:

$$U = .8 \times \sqrt{150000} + .2 \times \sqrt{0} = 309.8387$$

With the risky portfolio:

$$U = .7 \times \sqrt{114,000} + .3 \times \sqrt{76,000} = 319.0515$$

Therefore, in this case the client will prefer to take the risky portfolio.

18. This problem has interesting implications:
    With the annuity:

$$U = .8 \times \sqrt{150,000 - 20,000} + .2 \times \sqrt{0} = 288.4441$$

With the risky portfolio:

$$U = .7 \times \sqrt{114,000 - 20,000} + .3 \times \sqrt{76,000 - 20,000} = 285.6089$$

Naturally this Problem was designed to flip the answer relative to Problem 16, but the interesting part is that none of the outcomes impinge on the floor. The floor is important because "happiness" depends on how far off of the floor the client can jump. That the insurance contract exceeds the floor, even with the 20 percent deadweight loss for mortality, is less important in this case, than the risky portfolio's possibility of coming too close to the floor for the client's comfort. Certainty, by itself, can be a motivator.

19. With the inclusion of credit risk, the utility of the insurance contract becomes the following:

$$U = \left[.99 \left(.8 \times \sqrt{150,000 - 20,000} \right) + .01 \left(\sqrt{(0)} \right) \right] .2 \times \sqrt{0}$$
$$= 285.5597$$

For a client extremely concerned about credit risk, a lower floor constructed with treasury strips may be preferred even to a highly rated corporate obligation. Credit risk, particularly in the wake of AIG, is something about which clients are more acutely aware than would have been so previously.

20. Using the formulas for the mean and standard deviation of the process give:

$$\text{Expected}[V_T] = V_0 \times e^{rT} = \$100,000 \times e^{.5} = \$164,872$$

$$\sigma_{V_T} = V_0 \sqrt{e^{2rT}\left(e^{T\sigma^2} - 1\right)} = \$100,000 \sqrt{e\left(e^{.0025} - 1\right)} = \$8,249$$

Note that the standard deviation is roughly 5% of the expectation.

To find the $Z = \pm 1.645$ and the ± 2.33 values we use the formula for the process itself:

$$V_T = \$100,000 \begin{cases} e^{\left(.02 - \frac{.01^2}{2}\right)25 - .01 \times 1.645\sqrt{25}} \\ e^{\left(.02 - \frac{.01^2}{2}\right)25 + .01 \times 1.645\sqrt{25}} \end{cases}$$

$$= \begin{cases} \$151,664 \\ \$178,783 \end{cases}$$

$$V_T = \$100,000 \begin{cases} e^{\left(.02 - \frac{.01^2}{2}\right)25 - .01 \times 2.33\sqrt{25}} \\ e^{\left(.02 - \frac{.01^2}{2}\right)25 + .01 \times 2.33\sqrt{25}} \end{cases}$$

$$= \begin{cases} \$146,558 \\ \$185,012 \end{cases}$$

With changes in the price level following a lognormal process, the distribution of future price levels is skewed to the right—slightly higher inflation cumulates to a much higher price level than the corresponding results for slightly lower inflation.

21. The expected value of the portfolio 25 years from now is

$$\text{Expected}[V_T] = V_0 \times e^{rT} = \$1,000,000 \times e^{25 \times (.08)} = \$7,389,056$$

If the -1 or -1.645 standard deviation down events occur and the distribution is correct, then the outcomes will be

$$V_T = \$1,000,000 \begin{cases} e^{\left(.08 - \frac{.12^2}{2}\right)25 - .12 \times 1.645\sqrt{25}} \\ e^{\left(.08 - \frac{.12^2}{2}\right)25 - .12 \times 1\sqrt{25}} \end{cases}$$

$$= \begin{cases} \$2,300,209 \\ \$3,387,188 \end{cases}$$

The realized rates of return in these two cases are given by

$$\frac{Ln(\$2,300,209)}{25} = 3.33\%$$

and

$$\frac{Ln(\$3,387,188)}{25} = 4.88\%$$

22. The expected value of the portfolio 25 years from now is

$$\text{Expected}[V_T] = V_0 \times e^{rT} = \$1,000,000 \times e^{25 \times (3\% + 1.25 \times 5\%)} = \$10,099,642$$

If the -1 or -1.645 standard deviation down events occur and the distribution is correct, then the outcomes will be

$$V_T = \$1,000,000 \begin{cases} e^{\left(.0925 - \frac{.15^2}{2}\right)25 - .15 \times 1.645\sqrt{25}} \\ e^{\left(.0925 - \frac{.15^2}{2}\right)25 - .15 \times 1\sqrt{25}} \end{cases}$$

$$= \begin{cases} \$2,219,984 \\ \$3,601,138 \end{cases}$$

The realized rates of return in these two cases are given by

$$\frac{Ln(\$2,219,984)}{25} = 3.19\%$$

and

$$\frac{Ln(\$3,601,138)}{25} = 5.13\%$$

23. The portfolio in Problem 21 has a higher beta than the portfolio in Problem 20 and so it achieves a higher expected return and has a higher expected portfolio value. However, the risk is also going up. Using this type of market model, the volatility is proportional to beta but the expected return is growing less than proportionately with beta. It is true that in long-horizon lognormal models eventually the expected return dominates the volatility, but even the well-behaved lognormal model suggests that the change may lead to lower outcomes, even in the long run; switching to a higher return comes at a price in terms of risk.

Both the book and the workbook have more to say about the idea of taking more risk to dig out of a hole in Chapter 15.

24. We solve this one in somewhat gory detail because both the specific formula and the notion of using common spreadsheets to mass-customize portfolios will be used again in Chapter 7.

V	1000000.00
P	100000.00
r	0.04
M	1.00
g	0.00
r/M	0.04
g/M	0.00
1 + g/M	1.00
1 + r/M	1.04
V/P	10.00
V/P(r/M − g/M)	0.40
V/P(r/M − g/M)/(1 + g/M)	0.40
Ln(1 − V/P(r/M − g/M)/(1 + g/M))	−0.51
Ln((1 + g/M)/(1 + r/M))	−0.04
Result	13.02

With payments of 25,000 per quarter and an annual growth rate of 3%, the annuity will last 10.5 years.

V	1000000.00
P	25000.00
r	0.04
M	4.00
g	0.03
r/M	0.0100
g/M	0.0075
1 + g/M	1.0075
1 + r/M	1.0100
V/P	40.00
V/P(r/M − g/M)	0.10
V/P(r/M − g/M)/(1 + g/M)	0.099256
Ln(1 − V/P(r/M − g/M)/(1 + g/M))	−0.10453
Ln((1 + g/M)/(1 + r/M))	−0.00248
Result	10.54

CHAPTER 3

The Importance of Lifestyle Flooring

1. Using the information available and a balance sheet template, we develop the following balance sheet for the Piniella family:

Assets		Liabilities	
Human capital	$1,750,000	PV of future consumption	
		Mortgage	$350,000
Financial capital		Preretirement	$750,000
Portfolio	$500,000	consumption	
House	$600,000	Retirement	$1,100,000
		consumption	
		PV of desired	
		bequest	
Social capital			
		Discretionary	
		wealth	
			$650,000
Total	$2,850,000		$2,850,000

Notice that the amount available in discretionary wealth is the balancing amount that keeps the total on the left side of the balance sheet equal to the total on the right side.

2. The client earns $100,000 per year, just got paid, and consumes $65,000 per year. To construct the balance sheet we first calculate the PV of future earnings and preretirement consumption. We use a risk-free rate to discount consumption needs, but the risk-adjusted rate for discounting future earnings:

Age	PV(100 K, 4%)	PV(65 K, 3%)
53		$65,000
54	$96,154	$63,107
55	$92,456	$61,269
56	$88,900	$59,484
57	$85,480	$57,752
58	$82,193	$56,070
59	$79,031	$54,436
60	$75,992	$52,851
61	$73,069	$51,312
62	$70,259	$49,817
63	$67,556	$48,366
64	$64,958	$46,957
65	$62,460	$45,590
Total	$938,507	$712,010

Next we want to fit the information into the balance sheet template:

Assets	Liabilities
Human capital	PV of future consumption
Financial capital	PV of desired bequest
Social capital	Discretionary wealth
Total	Total

Using the data provided, we can begin with the following starter set of data:

Assets		Liabilities	
Human capital	$938,507	PV of future consumption	
		Mortgage	$400,000
Financial capital	$400,000	Preretirement consumption	$712,010
		PV of desired bequest	
Social capital	$1,000,000	Discretionary wealth	$1,226,497
Total	$2,338,507		$2,338,507

3. If the client's income is expected to rise by 10 percent per year, then the new PV of earnings will be given by the following:

Age	PV(100K, 4%)
53	
54	$105,769
55	$111,871
56	$118,325
57	$125,152
58	$132,372
59	$140,009
60	$148,086
61	$156,630
62	$165,666
63	$175,224
64	$185,333
65	$196,025
Total	$1,760,464

The balance sheet corresponding to the change is the following:

Assets		Liabilities	
Human capital PV earnings	$1,760,464	PV of future consumption Mortgage	$400,000
Financial capital Portfolio	$400,000	Preretirement consumption PV of desired	$712,010
Home	$1,000,000	bequest	
Social capital		Discretionary wealth	$2,048,454
Total	$3,160,464		$3,160,464

The points of this problem are that it is sometimes reasonable to factor in assumptions about the growth of future earnings in a career arc; future earnings are a substantial component of most client balance sheets; growth in earnings can have a substantial impact on client balance sheets.

4. The solution can be found either analytically or using a simple spreadsheet. Using portfolio wealth only:

Portfolio wealth = Income $\times$ PV$_{\text{Lump sum}}$ (12, 3%) $\times$ PV$_{\text{Annuity}}$ (20, 3%)

$\Rightarrow$

$$\text{Income} = \left(\frac{\text{Portfolio wealth}}{\text{PV}_{\text{Lump sum}}(12, 3\%) \times \text{PV}_{\text{Annuity}}(20, 3\%)} \right)$$

$$\text{Income} = \left(\frac{\$400,000}{10.43} \right) = \$38,333$$

5. Using the information in Problems 1 and 2. Analytically, the problem is to find a solution to the following:

Discretionary wealth = Income $\times$ PV$_{\text{Lump sum}}$ (12, 3%) $\times$ PV$_{\text{Annuity}}$ (20, 3%)

$\Rightarrow$

$$\text{Income} = \left(\frac{\text{Discretionary wealth}}{\text{PV}_{\text{Lump sum}}(12, 3\%) \times \text{PV}_{\text{Annuity}}(20, 3\%)} \right)$$

$$\text{Income} = \left(\frac{\text{Discretionary wealth}}{10.43} \right)$$

For the discretionary wealth in Problem 1, the income level is \$1,226,497/10.43 = \$196,311.

For the discretionary wealth in Problem 2, the income level is \$2,048,454/10.43 = \$196,311.

Note that so far we have ignored the likely impact of inflation.

6. The present value of savings is \$93,851. However, it is already accounted for in our balance sheet. Adding the savings to the balance sheet would be double counting.

7. The inflation-adjusted dollar requires $(1 + i)^N$ dollars. For inflation running at 2 percent, then at 20 years and 40 years, respectively, the client will need \$1.81 and \$3.26.

8. If discretionary wealth is \$2,000,000, then the task is to find the constant real income that can be sustained in retirement if inflation runs at 2 percent per year. We break this problem into two parts. The first is the 20-year annuity during retirement which then is PV'ed as a lump sum to present day.

$$\text{Discretionary wealth} = \text{Income} \times PV_{\text{Lump sum}}^{\text{Inflation adjusted}}(12, 4\%) \times$$
$$PV_{\text{Annuity}}^{\text{Inflation adjusted}}(20, 4\%)$$

$$\Rightarrow$$

$$\text{Income} = \left(\frac{\text{Discretionary wealth}}{13.00178} \right) = \$153,825.12$$

9. Augmenting the balance sheet obtained in Problem 2, the consumption required each year will be the following:

Age	Consumption	PV	Subtotals
53	$65,000	$65,000	
54	$66,300	$64,369	
55	$67,626	$63,744	
56	$68,979	$63,125	
57	$70,358	$62,512	
58	$71,765	$61,905	
59	$73,201	$61,304	
60	$74,665	$60,709	
61	$76,158	$60,120	
62	$77,681	$59,536	
63	$79,235	$58,958	
64	$80,819	$58,386	
65	$82,436	$57,819	$797,487
66	$84,084	$57,257	
67	$85,766	$56,702	
68	$87,481	$56,151	
69	$89,231	$55,606	
70	$91,016	$55,066	
71	$92,836	$54,531	
72	$94,693	$54,002	
73	$96,587	$53,478	
74	$98,518	$52,958	
75	$100,489	$52,444	
76	$102,498	$51,935	
77	$104,548	$51,431	
78	$106,639	$50,932	
79	$108,772	$50,437	
80	$110,948	$49,947	
81	$113,167	$49,462	

Age	Consumption	PV	Subtotals
82	$115,430	$48,982	
83	$117,739	$48,507	
84	$120,093	$48,036	
85	$122,495	$47,569	$1,045,434

The results can be placed into our balance sheet template and provide the answer for discretionary wealth of $917,543:

Assets		Liabilities	
Human capital	$1,760,464	PV of future consumption	
		Mortgage	$400,000
Financial capital		Preretirement	$797,487
Portfolio	$400,000	consumption	
House	$1,000,000	Postretirement	$1,045,434
		consumption	
		PV of desired	
		bequest	
Social capital		Discretionary	$917,543
		wealth	
Total	$3,160,464		$3,160,464

10. If the client wants to keep the house, then the value of the home comes off the table for calculating assets to be monetized and discretionary wealth. The easiest way to account for this is by taking the value of the home on the asset side and creating a contra-asset for the infeasibility of a sale. That takes the value of the housing out of consideration for the time being; but it records a value that can be utilized if the client changes their decision. Using the numbers from Problem 9, here is an example of how one might handle such a case. Since there is no FASB (Financial Accounting Standards Board) equivalent for economic balance sheets, there is no unique rule, just rules of thumb.

Note that in this example, eliminating housing from the "held for sale" category wipes out the discretionary wealth. The client may be quite content with the decision to stay in the same home or unaware of the consequences. The adviser needs to understand what aspects of their lifestyle that the client most deeply values. The client may be willing to delay retirement, reconsider a home sale, or perhaps rethink some of what are currently listed as needs.

Assets		Liabilities	
Human capital	$1,760,464	PV of future consumption	
		Mortgage	$400,000
Financial capital		Preretirement	$797,487
Portfolio	$400,000	consumption	
House	$1,000,000	Retirement consumption	$1,045,434
PV of future housing provided	$1,000,000	PV of desired bequest	
Social capital			
		Discretionary wealth	$(82,457)
Total	$2,160,464		$2,160,464

11. Without some changes, the client's plan to consume at a real rate of $100,000 is not feasible. It implies a negative value for discretionary wealth—there just isn't enough wealth to support that high of a lifestyle securely.

Assets		Liabilities	
Human capital	$1,760,464	PV of future consumption	
		Mortgage	$400,000
Financial capital		Preretirement	$1,226,903
Portfolio	$400,000	consumption	
House	$1,000,000	Retirement consumption	$1,608,360
		PV of desired bequest	
Social capital			
		Discretionary wealth	$(74,800)
Total	$3,160,464		$3,160,464

12. If the client is in a position to defer retirement for a year, then the lifestyle from Problem 10 becomes feasible. The other two recommended

options would have been to monetize mortality or rethink the lifestyle. (In Chapter 15's problems, we address the reason that taking more risk is not a recommended approach for digging out of a hole.)

Assets		Liabilities	
Human capital	$1,967,798	PV of future consumption	
		Mortgage	$400,000
Financial capital		Preretirement consumption	$1,314,992
Portfolio	$400,000		
House	$1,000,000	Retirement consumption	$1,520,272
		PV of desired bequest	
Social capital			
		Discretionary wealth	$132,535
Total	$3,367,798		$3,367,798

13. For someone with a $2,000,000 portfolio, a $1,000,000 house, and no debt, the wealth available for consumption will be $3,000,000. Consuming at the rate of 2.5 percent per year means that consumption will be $75,000 per year.

14. If the portfolio falls by 40 percent, the new wealth will be $2,200,000 and consumption will become $55,000—a decline of nearly 27 percent. The different groups working versus the elderly are each sensitive to different phenomena. In either case, the dollar sensitivity of consumption is greatest for the factor that is the largest component of economic wealth.

15. There is no impact on the current balance sheet and wealth is unchanged. What has changed is the probability distribution of portfolio values in future balance sheets.

16. This client has a present value of consumption that cannot be maintained without monetizing mortality; ignoring all of the complications that make people interesting, the answer is true. However, there are circumstances such as dependent children, an expectation of premature death, or being highly averse to credit risk, that make the answer uncertain.

17. Clients who can fully fund their retirements may still choose to annuitize all or part of their floor. Annuities offer tax deferral and simplicity that may be attractive even for those who have no need to monetize their mortality. Furthermore, with death benefits, insurance products offer advantages as mechanisms for intergenerational wealth transfer.

CHAPTER 4

Monetizing Mortality
Annuities and Longevity Insurance

1. $PV(30 \text{ years}, 4\%) = \left(\dfrac{1}{1.04}\right)^{30} = 0.308319$

2. There are no death benefits in this case, therefore,

$$PV = Pr(\text{Alive}) \times PV(30 \text{ years}, 4\%) + Pr(\text{Not alive}) \times 0$$
$$= 0.3 \times 0.308319 = \$0.0925$$

3. Assuming the client's survival, the yield to maturity (Ytm) is given by

$$\$0.0925 = \left(\dfrac{1}{1 + \text{Ytm}}\right)^{30}$$

$$\Rightarrow$$

$$0.0925^{\left(\frac{1}{30}\right)} = \left(\dfrac{1}{1 + \text{Ytm}}\right)$$

$$\Rightarrow$$

$$\text{Ytm} = \left(\dfrac{1}{0.0925^{\left(\frac{1}{30}\right)}}\right) - 1 = 8.258\%$$

4. The present value is now

$$PV = Pr(\text{Alive}) \times PV(30 \text{ years}, 4\%) + Pr(\text{Not alive}) \times 10\% \times PV(30 \text{ years}, 4\%)$$
$$= (0.3 + 0.7 \times 10\%) \times 0.308319 = \$0.1141$$

The yield to maturity becomes:

$$Ytm = \left(\frac{1}{0.1141^{\left(\frac{1}{30} \right)}} \right) - 1 = 7.504\%$$

Even a small death benefit, and even if the payment is deferred, can have a substantial impact on the yield of a longevity contract.

5. Life expectancy represents the length of the average life. A slight skewness to the distribution aside, roughly half of your clients will live past the age of life expectancy.

6. Using 1.645 standard units implies that 5 percent of clients will survive beyond the following:

$$85 \text{ years} + 1.645 \times 6 \text{ years} \approx 95 \text{ years}$$

7. Some would attribute surrender charges as a way to transfer the costly nature of an individual contracting to those who will seek to change their contracts. A more likely explanation is that the act of attempting to surrender conveys valuable information to the insurance company. A person who seeks to surrender a policy may be signaling that he or she now expects to die sooner than thought and that the surrendered value of the policy exceeds the value of holding the policy. To the insurance company, that means that someone who would likely benefit the risk pool is opting out of the pool; the people who want out are the ones that the insurance company wants in. The company will seek to mitigate the impact on the pool by charging a fee for reversal, surrender charges.

8. For the risk-free zero-coupon bond:

$$V = \frac{\$1,000}{1.06} = \$943.40$$

For XYZ's debt:

$$V = \frac{\$1,000}{1.063} = \$940.73$$

9. The policies cost \$917.22 and only pay if alive. If p represents the probability of survival then we can write

$$\$917.22 = p \times \$940.73 + (1-p) \times \$0$$

$$\Rightarrow p = \frac{\$917.22}{\$940.73} = 0.975$$

The probability of survival is 97.5 percent and the probability of death is 2.5%.

10. The recovery rate is assumed to be 40 percent. We can rewrite the claim as the following:

$$V = \text{pr(No default)} \times \text{PV(Face, risk free)} + \text{pr(Default)} \times \text{PV(Face, risk free)}$$

$$\$940.73 = \text{pr(No default)} \times \$943.40 + \text{pr(Default)} \times 40\% \times \$943.40$$

$$\Rightarrow \text{pr(Default)} = \frac{\$940.73 - \$943.40}{\$943.40 \times (40\% - 1)} = 0.005$$

As an aside, a 40 percent recovery rate is the figure that is often assumed by debt traders. It is so common that at many of even the largest firms, the 40 percent recovery rate is hard-coded into software. Naturally, the current crisis has shown this assumption to be something other than a rule. Even Lehman Brothers, which had used the 40 percent recovery rate internally for valuation and risk purposes, found its own debt fetching below 10 percent after the company's default.

11. The relevant rate for comparison is the rate on the insurance company's straight debt. We can solve this either by brute force or by using the formula that was developed in Chapter 2 of the workbook:

$$N = \frac{1}{M} \left(\frac{\text{Ln}\left(1 - \dfrac{V}{P}\left(\dfrac{\dfrac{r}{M} - \dfrac{g}{M}}{1 + \dfrac{g}{M}}\right)\right)}{\text{Ln}\left(\dfrac{1 + \dfrac{g}{M}}{1 + \dfrac{r}{M}}\right)} \right)$$

With $M = 1$ and $g = 0$, the above expression reduces to:

$$N = \left(\frac{\text{Ln}\left(1 - \dfrac{V}{P}\left(\dfrac{r}{1}\right)\right)}{\text{Ln}\left(\dfrac{1}{1+r}\right)} \right) = \frac{\text{Ln}\left(1 - \dfrac{\$573,496.10}{\$50,000}\left(\dfrac{0.06}{1}\right)\right)}{\text{Ln}\left(\dfrac{1}{1.06}\right)} = 20 \text{ years}$$

12. With inflation running at 3 percent per year, the lifestyle is imperiled as soon as Lifestyle $\times$ (1 + inflation)^N $\leq$ pmt. In this case, that would be when \$30,000 $\times$ (1.03)^N $\geq$ \$50,000:

$$\Rightarrow N \geq \frac{\text{Ln}\left(\dfrac{\$50,000}{\$30,000}\right)}{\text{Ln}(1.03)} = 17.28$$

13. We examine this in the context of the previous example. For the first 17 years, the annuity provides a surplus that can be reinvested in a money-market account that "should" roughly keep pace with inflation, after that the surplus account will be drawn down to augment the erosion of purchasing power inherent in the constant payments. In a purely mechanical sense, this type of scheme does afford some measure of protection as the following example demonstrates:

Year	Annuity Payment	Lifestyle Needs	Surplus Account
1	\$50,000	\$30,900	\$19,100
2	\$50,000	\$31,827	\$37,846
3	\$50,000	\$32,782	\$56,200
4	\$50,000	\$33,765	\$74,120
5	\$50,000	\$34,778	\$91,566
6	\$50,000	\$35,822	\$108,491
7	\$50,000	\$36,896	\$124,850
8	\$50,000	\$38,003	\$140,592
9	\$50,000	\$39,143	\$155,667
10	\$50,000	\$40,317	\$170,019
11	\$50,000	\$41,527	\$183,593
12	\$50,000	\$42,773	\$196,328
13	\$50,000	\$44,056	\$208,161
14	\$50,000	\$45,378	\$219,029
15	\$50,000	\$46,739	\$228,860
16	\$50,000	\$48,141	\$237,585
17	\$50,000	\$49,585	\$245,127
18	\$50,000	\$51,073	\$251,408
19	\$50,000	\$52,605	\$256,345
20	\$50,000	\$54,183	\$259,852
21	\$50,000	\$55,809	\$261,839
22	\$50,000	\$57,483	\$262,211
23	\$50,000	\$59,208	\$260,869
24	\$50,000	\$60,984	\$257,712
25	\$50,000	\$62,813	\$252,630

Year	Annuity Payment	Lifestyle Needs	Surplus Account
26	$50,000	$64,698	$245,511
27	$50,000	$66,639	$236,238
28	$50,000	$68,638	$224,687
29	$50,000	$70,697	$210,731
30	$50,000	$72,818	$194,235
31	$50,000	$75,002	$175,059
32	$50,000	$77,252	$153,058
33	$50,000	$79,570	$128,080
34	$50,000	$81,957	$99,965
35	$50,000	$84,416	$68,549
36	$50,000	$86,948	$33,657
37	$50,000	$89,557	$(4,890)

In this example, the client can forestall inflation for 36 years. However, the mechanical appeal is somewhat deceptive. At a 5 percent inflation rate, the protection lasts 22 years. Keeping the surplus locked up is vastly more difficult than the arithmetic can show. Furthermore, this approach is likely to be more expensive than purchasing an inflation-adjusted annuity because the extra payments in the early years do not fully monetize the client's declining probability of continued survival.

CHAPTER 5

Flooring with Capital Markets Products

1a. The note the client purchases is $900,000 in notional value of flooring.

1b. We can use the formula developed in Chapter 2 of the workbook:

$$PV_{\text{Annuity}}(N, r) = \frac{1}{r}\left(1 - \left(\frac{1}{1+r}\right)^N\right)$$

This tells us PV_{Annuity}(30 years, 4%) = 17.29203. The solution is given by the annuity factor multiplied by the payment level 17.29203 × $30,000 = $518,761.

2. Use the following table as a check of the formula in the problems section:

Pay Date	Annual Rate	Price
6 months	1.55%	$99.23
12 months	1.60%	$98.44
18 months	1.65%	$97.64
24 months	1.70%	$96.81
30 months	1.75%	$95.98
36 months	1.80%	$95.12
42 months	1.85%	$94.25
48 months	1.90%	$93.36
54 months	1.95%	$92.46
60 months	2.00%	$91.54
66 months	2.05%	$90.61
72 months	2.10%	$89.67
78 months	2.15%	$88.72
84 months	2.20%	$87.75

(*Continued*)

Pay Date	Annual Rate	Price
90 months	2.25%	$86.78
96 months	2.30%	$85.79
102 months	2.35%	$84.79
108 months	2.40%	$83.79
114 months	2.45%	$82.78
120 months	2.50%	$81.75
126 months	2.55%	$80.72
132 months	2.60%	$79.69
138 months	2.65%	$78.65
144 months	2.70%	$77.60
150 months	2.75%	$76.55
156 months	2.80%	$75.49
162 months	2.85%	$74.43
168 months	2.90%	$73.36
174 months	2.95%	$72.30
180 months	3.00%	$71.23
186 months	3.05%	$70.16
192 months	3.10%	$69.09
198 months	3.15%	$68.02
204 months	3.20%	$66.95
210 months	3.25%	$65.88
216 months	3.30%	$64.81
222 months	3.35%	$63.74
228 months	3.40%	$62.67
234 months	3.45%	$61.61
240 months	3.50%	$60.55
246 months	3.55%	$59.50
252 months	3.60%	$58.44
258 months	3.65%	$57.40
264 months	3.70%	$56.35
270 months	3.75%	$55.32
276 months	3.80%	$54.28
282 months	3.85%	$53.26
288 months	3.90%	$52.24
294 months	3.95%	$51.23
300 months	4.00%	$50.22
306 months	4.05%	$49.23
312 months	4.10%	$48.24
318 months	4.15%	$47.26
324 months	4.20%	$46.29

Pay Date	Annual Rate	Price
330 months	4.25%	$45.32
336 months	4.30%	$44.37
342 months	4.35%	$43.42
348 months	4.40%	$42.49
354 months	4.45%	$41.57
360 months	4.50%	$40.65

3. The new notional will be $1,000 × 1.04 = $1,040, the coupon rate will remain unchanged at 3 percent, but the coupon paid will be based on the new notional at 3% × $1,040 × 0.5 = $15.60 (remember, the coupon is paid semiannually).

4. Yes, TIPS with notional values above $1,000 can adjust downward. In this case, the notional on the security will be adjusted to $1,060 × 0.96 = $1,017.60 and the coupon will be adjusted downward to $15.26 (semiannually).

5. For the risk-free debt, the price will be the following:

$$V = \frac{\$1,000}{1.02} = \$980.39$$

The prices of ABC's and DEF's debt will be the following:

$$V_{ABC} = \frac{\$1,000}{1.023} = \$977.52$$

$$V_{DEF} = \frac{\$1,000}{1.034} = \$967.12$$

6. The one-year default probabilities for ABC and DEF are 0.587 percent and 2.708 percent, respectively. The answer is found by applying the following formula:

$$V = \text{pr}(\text{No default}) \times \text{PV}\left(\text{Face}, r_f\right) + \text{pr}(\text{Default}) \times \text{PV}\left(\text{Pmt in default}, r_f\right)$$

$$\Rightarrow \text{pr}(\text{Default}) = 1 - \frac{V - \text{PV}\left(\text{Pmt in default}, r_f\right)}{\text{PV}\left(\text{Face}, r_f\right) - \text{PV}\left(\text{Pmt in default}, r_f\right)}$$

As we would expect, the default probability is higher for the firm with the higher credit spread.

7. At the higher risk-free rate, the value of ABC's and DEF's debt become, respectively:

$$V_{ABC} = \frac{\$1,000}{1.063} = \$940.73$$

$$V_{DEF} = \frac{\$1,000}{1.074} = \$931.10$$

Using the formula given in the answer to Problem 6, the new default probabilities are 0.564% for ABC and 2.607% for DEF. We note that for constant credit spreads, default probabilities are inversely related to the level of rates. To some extent this is an artifact of the compounding, but ought to be stored somewhere in the back of your mind.

8. Spread changes imply changes in the market's perception of the probability of a debt issue defaulting and/or the recovery rate in the event of a default. The reliability of flooring is a paramount concern, meaning that advisers need to pay attention to spreads and not just ratings and also need to pay better attention to the mitigation of credit risk. (What is to happen to retirees who had a significant exposure to the debt of GM, Lehman, Chrysler, and the like?)

9. The cost of the flooring at $20,000 per half year for the client with the given yield curve and inflation expectations would be $732,843. Observe the following table, which provides the cost for both level payments of $20,000 and the payment stream adjusted for expected inflation:

Pay Date (Months)	Price	Payment	Cost for Level Payments	Payment	Cost with Adjustment
6	0.9847	$20,000	$19,695	$20,200	$19,892
12	0.9692	$20,000	$19,385	$20,402	$19,774
18	0.9535	$20,000	$19,070	$20,606	$19,648
24	0.9376	$20,000	$18,751	$20,812	$19,513
30	0.9214	$20,000	$18,429	$21,020	$19,369
36	0.9051	$20,000	$18,103	$21,230	$19,216
42	0.8887	$20,000	$17,774	$21,443	$19,056
48	0.8721	$20,000	$17,443	$21,657	$18,888
54	0.8554	$20,000	$17,109	$21,874	$18,712
60	0.8387	$20,000	$16,773	$22,092	$18,528

Pay Date (Months)	Price	Payment	Cost for Level Payments	Payment	Cost with Adjustment
66	0.8218	$20,000	$16,437	$22,313	$18,338
72	0.8049	$20,000	$16,098	$22,537	$18,140
78	0.7880	$20,000	$15,760	$22,762	$17,936
84	0.7710	$20,000	$15,420	$22,989	$17,725
90	0.7541	$20,000	$15,081	$23,219	$17,509
96	0.7371	$20,000	$14,742	$23,452	$17,286
102	0.7202	$20,000	$14,404	$23,686	$17,058
108	0.7033	$20,000	$14,066	$23,923	$16,825
114	0.6865	$20,000	$13,730	$24,162	$16,587
120	0.6697	$20,000	$13,395	$24,404	$16,344
126	0.6531	$20,000	$13,062	$24,648	$16,097
132	0.6365	$20,000	$12,731	$24,894	$15,846
138	0.6201	$20,000	$12,402	$25,143	$15,591
144	0.6038	$20,000	$12,076	$25,395	$15,333
150	0.5876	$20,000	$11,753	$25,649	$15,072
156	0.5716	$20,000	$11,433	$25,905	$14,808
162	0.5558	$20,000	$11,116	$26,164	$14,542
168	0.5401	$20,000	$10,803	$26,426	$14,273
174	0.5246	$20,000	$10,493	$26,690	$14,003
180	0.5094	$20,000	$10,187	$26,957	$13,731
186	0.4943	$20,000	$9,886	$27,227	$13,458
192	0.4794	$20,000	$9,589	$27,499	$13,184
198	0.4648	$20,000	$9,296	$27,774	$12,909
204	0.4504	$20,000	$9,008	$28,052	$12,634
210	0.4362	$20,000	$8,724	$28,332	$12,358
216	0.4223	$20,000	$8,445	$28,615	$12,083
222	0.4086	$20,000	$8,172	$28,902	$11,809
228	0.3951	$20,000	$7,903	$29,191	$11,534
234	0.3820	$20,000	$7,639	$29,482	$11,261
240	0.3690	$20,000	$7,381	$29,777	$10,989
246	0.3564	$20,000	$7,128	$30,075	$10,719
252	0.3440	$20,000	$6,880	$30,376	$10,450
258	0.3319	$20,000	$6,638	$30,680	$10,182
264	0.3201	$20,000	$6,401	$30,986	$9,917
270	0.3085	$20,000	$6,170	$31,296	$9,655
276	0.2972	$20,000	$5,944	$31,609	$9,394
282	0.2862	$20,000	$5,724	$31,925	$9,136

(*Continued*)

Pay Date (Months)	Price	Payment	Cost for Level Payments	Payment	Cost with Adjustment
288	0.2754	$20,000	$5,509	$32,245	$8,881
294	0.2650	$20,000	$5,299	$32,567	$8,629
300	0.2548	$20,000	$5,096	$32,893	$8,380

10. If the client wants to add on a longevity bullet payable in 25 years, then we can use the proceding table to compute the answer. A current level of $400,000 adjusted for expected inflation would be 20 times greater than the $8,380 it would cost for the present value of the inflation-adjusted $20,000 semiannual payment. With a survival probability of 20 percent, the cost would be $20 \times \$8,380.30 \times 0.20 = \$33,521.20$.

11. Under the assumption that rates will remain at 5 percent long enough to lock in flooring for ages 81 through 90 would require $17,866. Since rates are uncertain, the worst case would be if we stacked an extra $100,000 in notional at year 80. The cost in today's prices to set funds available for years 81 through 90 would be $100,000 \times 1.05^{-30} = \$23,138$. As later year's debt becomes available for purchase we could whittle down the stack and roll out the flooring. This process, not surprisingly, is called a *stack and roll hedge*.

Building Retirement Income Portfolios

1. With a yield to maturity of 5.51 percent, the cost of the bullet payment will be $0.20 on the dollar $\left(\dfrac{1}{1.0551}\right)^{30} = 0.2000$. Therefore, for $10,000 in notional the client will pay $2,000. The allocation within the IRA will be $\dfrac{\$2,000}{\$5,000} = 0.40$ to flooring and 0.60 to upside. The expected return on the portfolio will be 0.4 × .0551 + 0.6 × 0.10 = 8.204%.

2. The expected value of the first year's contribution at the end of the 30 years will be Expected[V_T]=$3,000 × $e^{(0.09531)30}$ = $52,347.92. The expected value of the first year's contribution at the end of 30 years will be $62,347.92.

3. Sticking with the plan, by age 65 the client is expected to have $22,000 per year in flooring out to age 95 ($12,000 per year in SSI, for life plus $10,000 per year in the flooring purchased within the IRA that covers ages 65 up to 95). The two main reasons to be wary of the estimate are that it requires that the client stick to the plan and that the cost of the 30-year bullets are to remain no higher than $2,000.

4. The client's plan requires annual deposits into the risky portfolio. The expectation can be found by summing the following terms:

$$\text{Expected}[V_T] = \$3,000 \times \left(e^{(0.9531)30} + e^{(0.9531)29} + \cdots + e^{(0.9531)1}\right)$$

Years of Exposure	Expected Growth	Incremental Saving	Net Expectation at Age 65
30	17.44930814	$3,000	$52,348
29	15.86301026	$3,000	$99,937
28	14.42092101	$3,000	$143,200
27	13.10993055	$3,000	$182,530
26	11.91812082	$3,000	$218,284
25	10.83465724	$3,000	$250,788
24	9.849690171	$3,000	$280,337
23	8.954265402	$3,000	$307,200
22	8.140242738	$3,000	$331,620
21	7.400222002	$3,000	$353,821
20	6.727475757	$3,000	$374,004
19	6.115888151	$3,000	$392,351
18	5.559899319	$3,000	$409,031
17	5.054454835	$3,000	$424,194
16	4.594959767	$3,000	$437,979
15	4.177236903	$3,000	$450,511
14	3.797488777	$3,000	$461,903
13	3.452263145	$3,000	$472,260
12	3.138421605	$3,000	$481,675
11	2.853111063	$3,000	$490,235
10	2.593737796	$3,000	$498,016
9	2.357943875	$3,000	$505,090
8	2.143585727	$3,000	$511,521
7	1.948714647	$3,000	$517,367
6	1.771559089	$3,000	$522,681
5	1.610508552	$3,000	$527,513
4	1.464098947	$3,000	$531,905
3	1.330999282	$3,000	$535,898
2	1.209999565	$3,000	$539,528
1	1.099999802	$3,000	$542,828

The expectation is that the client will have a risky portfolio worth $542,828 by the time of retirement.

5. The future value of the flooring account can be found either by brute force or by using the formula for the future value of an annuity. Using brute force, we arrive at the following total for the flooring account:

Age at Bond Maturity	Flooring Notionals	Value at Age 65
65	$10,000	$10,000
66	$10,000	$9,478
67	$10,000	$8,983
68	$10,000	$8,514
69	$10,000	$8,069
70	$10,000	$7,648
71	$10,000	$7,248
72	$10,000	$6,870
73	$10,000	$6,511
74	$10,000	$6,171
75	$10,000	$5,849
76	$10,000	$5,543
77	$10,000	$5,254
78	$10,000	$4,979
79	$10,000	$4,719
80	$10,000	$4,473
81	$10,000	$4,239
82	$10,000	$4,018
83	$10,000	$3,808
84	$10,000	$3,609
85	$10,000	$3,421
86	$10,000	$3,242
87	$10,000	$3,073
88	$10,000	$2,912
89	$10,000	$2,760
90	$10,000	$2,616
91	$10,000	$2,480
92	$10,000	$2,350
93	$10,000	$2,227
94	$10,000	$2,111
	Total	$153,176

The total of the two accounts, flooring plus upside, is expected to be $153,176 + $542,828 = 696,004.

6. The client is expected to draw $50,000, with $28,000 coming from the discretionary wealth component of the IRA account. Out of the $542,828 in the discretionary wealth portfolio, the client will be expected to draw 5.16 percent.

7. If the IRA withdrawals are taxed at 40 percent, then the after-tax value of the $38,000 withdrawal will be $(1 - .40) \times \$38,000 = \$22,800$.

8. For a continuous return equivalent to the 8.204 percent APR in Problem 1, we want to find x to solve the following:

$$8.204\% = e^x - 1$$
$$\Leftrightarrow 1.08204 = e^x$$
$$\Leftrightarrow x = \text{Ln}(1.08204) = .078848$$

9. Using an expected continuous return of 7.8848 percent would create an account with an expected value of $636,295.

Years of Exposure	Expected Growth	Incremental Saving	Net Expectation at Age 65
30	10.64872323	$5,000	$53,244
29	9.841341175	$5,000	$102,450
28	9.095174517	$5,000	$147,926
27	8.405581925	$5,000	$189,954
26	7.768273975	$5,000	$228,795
25	7.179286465	$5,000	$264,692
24	6.634955759	$5,000	$297,867
23	6.131895996	$5,000	$328,526
22	5.666978028	$5,000	$356,861
21	5.237309959	$5,000	$383,048
20	4.840219157	$5,000	$407,249
19	4.473235624	$5,000	$429,615
18	4.13407664	$5,000	$450,285
17	3.820632558	$5,000	$469,388
16	3.530953684	$5,000	$487,043
15	3.26323815	$5,000	$503,359
14	3.015820704	$5,000	$518,438
13	2.787162352	$5,000	$532,374
12	2.575840787	$5,000	$545,254
11	2.380541541	$5,000	$557,156
10	2.200049808	$5,000	$568,156
9	2.033242888	$5,000	$578,323
8	1.879083203	$5,000	$587,718
7	1.736611846	$5,000	$596,401
6	1.604942612	$5,000	$604,426
5	1.483256488	$5,000	$611,842
4	1.370796558	$5,000	$618,696
3	1.266863296	$5,000	$625,030
2	1.170810214	$5,000	$630,884
1	1.08203984	$5,000	$636,295

10. Using a continuous rate, $r = 7.88\%$, implies the expected portfolio to grow to $636,295. Without a flooring account, the client will be expecting to draw somewhere between $10,000 and $38,000 per year, implying a draw rate between $10,000/636,295 = 1.57\%$ and $38,000/636,295 = 5.97\%$.

11. In order to save $5,000 per year, the client will need to earn the amount Y such that $Y(1 - .4) = \$5,000$, that is, $Y = 5,000/.6 = \$8,333$.

12. The pretax yield on the instruments is 5.51 percent. The accreted value of zero-coupon bonds is taxed as ordinary income even though no actual cash changes hands during the year. The after-tax yield will therefore be $.0551 \times (1 - .40) = 3.306\%$. This means that the after-tax notional that will remain at maturity $= 2,000 \times 1.03306^{30} = \$5,306.36$.

13. The amount needed to make the after-tax income from the zero-coupon bond equal to $10,000 would cost $M(1 + .0551(1 - .4))^{30}$. That is, $M = \$10,000/(1.03306)^{30} = \$3,769$; the notional amount would be $\$3,769 \times (1.0551)^{30} = \$18,838$.

    $\$10,000/.6 = \$16,667$ would be the amount needed if the tax liability was incurred on the payment date rather than on an accrual basis.

14. We want the pretax earnings to be sufficient to provide $6,000 in flooring on a fully after-tax basis. This is a simple 60 percent of the answer to problem 13: $60\% \times \$3,769 = \$2,261$.

15. By the assumptions of the problem, the only taxes incurred would be capital gains taxes upon sale of the asset. At the end of 30 years, the after-tax expected value of the investment is:

$$\text{Expected}[V_T] = \$3,000 \times \left(e^{(0.09531)30} - 1\right) \times .9 + \$3,000 = \$47,413$$

16. Since the fully taxable account is taxed both before going in and on the way out (but at different rates), the pretax deposit saved (the amount of gross earnings that will be saved) must be sufficient such that the actual deposit, $D = .6$ (pretax deposit), has an expectation:

$$\text{Expected}[V_T] = (1 - .10)D \times \left(e^{(0.09531)30} - 1\right) = \$31,409$$

$$\Rightarrow D = \frac{\$31,409}{.9 \times \left(e^{(0.09531)30} - 1\right)} = \$2,122$$

But $\$2,122 = (1 - .4)$ pretax deposit. This means that the pretax savings must be at least $3,535 to achieve the expectation.

17. In this case, we want to find E such that $(1 - .6) \times E \times (1.0551)^{30} = 6,000$.

$$(1-.4)(1.0551)^{30} \times E = \$6,000$$
$$\Leftrightarrow E = \frac{\$6,000}{(1-.4)(1.0551)^{30}} = \$2,001$$

18. The goal is to now find D such that the Roth account equals the after-tax of the traditional IRA: $(1 - T_0)De^{.09531 \times 30} = \$53,244(1 - T_0)$. Since tax rates are the same at both the starting and ending points, then the timing of the taxation becomes irrelevant.

19. If there is an expectation for lower tax rates in the future, then a Traditional IRA is generally preferred over a Roth IRA. The converse is also true: An expectation of higher taxes in the future makes the Roth IRA the more attractive choice.

20. The client's liability is known and grows at the risk-free rate. After 20 years, the liability will have grown to \$903,056. The client wants to save enough so that the future value of an annuity growing at a 4 percent annual rate is at least \$903,056.

$$\$903,056 = \text{Pmt} \times \left(\frac{1.04^{21} - 1}{.04} \right) = \text{Pmt} \times 31.969$$
$$\Rightarrow \text{Pmt} = \$28,248$$

21. This plan poses risks to the client since the floor is not being covered with risk-free assets. There is the potential that the risky portfolio could underperform its expected minimum, even if that minimum is an all-time historical low. It may be a risk that the client is willing to take, but it is a risk nonetheless.

22. The cost of the annuity in 20 years will be \$773,500. This means that the implied growth rate can be found by calculating

$$\$773,500 = \$400,000 \times (1 + g)^{20}$$
$$\Rightarrow (1 + g)^{20} = \frac{773,500}{400,000}$$
$$\Rightarrow g = \frac{\text{Ln}\left(\dfrac{773,500}{400,000} \right)}{20} - 1 = 3.3\%$$

We also want to find the value of r such that the future value of an annuity of $30,000 over 21 years accrues to at least $773,500. Since $773,500 is roughly 25.78 × $30,000. We find the solution by noting that the result lies between 1 percent and 3 percent. By iteration, we find that the solution is 2 percent. This means that the client's risky portfolio needs to attain an average geometric growth rate of 2 percent to be able to purchase the annuity as a fall-back position in case of underperformance of the risky portfolio. Of course if the portfolio achieves more than 3.5 percent, then the client will have sufficient funds ($908,084) to have a choice of the flooring type whether insurance or capital markets.

CHAPTER 7

Creating Allocations for Constructing Practical Portfolios by Age and Lifestyle Needs

1. The easiest way to solve this problem is to use the formula for annuities calculating the value for a 29-year annuity and subtracting off a four-year annuity. However, to facilitate development of allocation tables in later problems we calculate the values long form in a spreadsheet.

Year	Payment	PV Factor	PV of Payment
1	$—	0.952380952	$—
2	$—	0.907029478	$—
3	$—	0.863837599	$—
4	$—	0.822702475	$—
5	$100,000	0.783526166	$78,353
6	$100,000	0.746215397	$74,622
7	$100,000	0.71068133	$71,068
8	$100,000	0.676839362	$67,684
9	$100,000	0.644608916	$64,461
10	$100,000	0.613913254	$61,391
11	$100,000	0.584679289	$58,468
12	$100,000	0.556837418	$55,684
13	$100,000	0.530321351	$53,032
14	$100,000	0.505067953	$50,507
15	$100,000	0.481017098	$48,102
16	$100,000	0.458111522	$45,811
17	$100,000	0.436296688	$43,630
18	$100,000	0.415520655	$41,552
19	$100,000	0.395733957	$39,573
20	$100,000	0.376889483	$37,689

(*Continued*)

Year	Payment	PV Factor	PV of Payment
21	$100,000	0.358942365	$35,894
22	$100,000	0.341849871	$34,185
23	$100,000	0.325571306	$32,557
24	$100,000	0.31006791	$31,007
25	$100,000	0.295302772	$29,530
26	$100,000	0.281240735	$28,124
27	$100,000	0.267848319	$26,785
28	$100,000	0.255093637	$25,509
29	$100,000	0.242946321	$24,295
	Total		$1,159,512

2. Using a slightly modified version of the formula that we created for Problems 23 and 24 in Chapter 2, we obtain the following:

$P/V\%$	8.00%
r	0.05
M	1.00
g	0.00
V/P	12.50
r/M	0.05
g/M	0.00
$1 + g/M$	1.00
$1 + r/M$	1.05
$V/P(r/M - g/M)$	0.63
$V/P(r/M - g/M)/(1 + g/M)$	0.63
$\mathrm{Ln}(1 - V/P(r/M - g/M)/(1 + g/M))$	−0.98
$\mathrm{Ln}((1 + g/M)/(1 + r/M))$	−0.05
Result	20.10

3. The center column of the table is the only part of the formula for annuity length that needs to be adapted to vary draw rates.

Draw Rates (P/V)	ln(1 − V/P(r/M − g/M)/ (1 + g/M))	Annuity Span in Years
5%	−∞	∞
6%	−1.79	36.72
7%	−1.25	25.68
8%	−0.98	20.10
9%	−0.81	16.62
10%	−0.69	14.21

Draw Rates (P/V)	ln(1 − V/P(r/M − g/M)/ (1 + g/M))	Annuity Span in Years
11%	−0.61	12.42
12%	−0.54	11.05
13%	−0.49	9.95
14%	−0.44	9.06
15%	−0.41	8.31

4. We now create the whole table for determination of how long ordinary annuities will pay out allowing variation in payout rates and growth rates in payouts:

Annuity Span in Years

Draw Rates (V/P)	0% Growth	1% Growth	2% Growth	3% Growth	4% Growth	5% Growth	6% Growth
5%	∞	40.44	30.61	25.56	22.32	20.00	18.23
6%	36.72	27.78	23.24	20.33	18.25	16.67	15.41
7%	25.68	21.48	18.80	16.89	15.44	14.29	13.34
8%	20.10	17.59	15.81	14.46	13.38	12.50	11.76
9%	16.62	14.93	13.65	12.64	11.81	11.11	10.52
10%	14.21	12.98	12.02	11.23	10.56	10.00	9.51
11%	12.42	11.49	10.73	10.10	9.56	9.09	8.68
12%	11.05	10.31	9.70	9.18	8.73	8.33	7.98
13%	9.95	9.35	8.85	8.41	8.03	7.69	7.39
14%	9.06	8.56	8.14	7.76	7.44	7.14	6.88
15%	8.31	7.89	7.53	7.21	6.92	6.67	6.43

5. We now make the table dynamic by allowing for deferral periods to be used. The deferral periods correspond to the length of time that the client has remaining until retirement withdrawals are set to begin:

Use $D = 0$ and compare with the previous table as a check.

Then use $D = 5$ for the following table:

Annuity Span in Years

Draw Rates (V/P)	0% Growth	1% Growth	2% Growth	3% Growth	4% Growth	5% Growth	6% Growth
5%	∞	84.10	39.31	29.01	23.54	20.00	17.46
6%	∞	41.64	28.85	22.91	19.23	16.67	14.74

(*Continued*)

Draw Rates (V/P)	0% Growth	1% Growth	2% Growth	3% Growth	4% Growth	5% Growth	6% Growth
7%	49.73	29.91	22.94	18.95	16.26	14.29	12.76
8%	32.75	23.67	19.09	16.17	14.08	12.50	11.24
9%	25.30	19.68	16.37	14.10	12.42	11.11	10.05
10%	20.83	16.88	14.33	12.51	11.11	10.00	9.09
11%	17.79	14.80	12.75	11.24	10.05	9.09	8.29
12%	15.55	13.19	11.49	10.20	9.17	8.33	7.63
13%	13.84	11.89	10.46	9.34	8.44	7.69	7.06
14%	12.47	10.84	9.60	8.62	7.81	7.14	6.57
15%	11.36	9.95	8.87	7.99	7.27	6.67	6.15

Notice that the entry for a draw rate of 6 percent and 0 percent growth has changed from 36.72 years without the deferral to an essentially infinite length if with only a five-year deferral. What is happening with the deferral is that it is effectively discounting the payoff percentage; and the lifespan of the annuity becomes infinite once the draw rate, or its present value, becomes equal to or lower than the discount rate. As the deferral horizon increases, more draw rates become infinitely sustainable. Along the other edge of the table, notice that as the growth rate exceeds the discount rate, then deferring the annuity shortens the lifespan of the annuity.

Use $D = 10$ for the following table:

Annuity Span in Years

Draw Rates (V/P)	0% Growth	1% Growth	2% Growth	3% Growth	4% Growth	5% Growth	6% Growth
5%	∞	∞	53.19	33.08	24.85	20.00	16.71
6%	∞	93.33	36.72	25.89	20.27	16.67	14.10
7%	∞	46.28	28.44	21.31	17.13	14.29	12.20
8%	∞	33.71	23.31	18.12	14.82	12.50	10.75
9%	48.23	26.95	19.80	15.76	13.07	11.11	9.61
10%	34.52	22.58	17.22	13.95	11.69	10.00	8.69
11%	27.64	19.49	15.25	12.52	10.57	9.09	7.92
12%	23.27	17.17	13.69	11.35	9.65	8.33	7.29
13%	20.19	15.36	12.42	10.39	8.87	7.69	6.74
14%	17.87	13.90	11.37	9.57	8.21	7.14	6.28
15%	16.05	12.70	10.48	8.87	7.64	6.67	5.87

6. Using the dynamic table with a 20-year deferral, the client can expect the growing annuity to last 33.55 years. This means that there is room to spare for building upside. Furthermore, the floor that is currently in place takes no advantage of the client's possibility to pool mortality risk and use an insurance-based annuity. By monetizing mortality, either with longevity insurance or a standard lifetime annuity, the client may find a solution that frees up more assets for creating upside potential.

7. The easiest way is to set up the entries so that the components of each cell represent Pmt as Pct $\times$ $(1 + g)^{(\text{Flow yr} - \text{Current age})}$. *Hint:* Keeping the payment and growth rates as references rather than placing values directly in the cells will make this table more flexible.

Flow Year	Current Age								
	35	40	45	50	55	60	65	70	75
65	2.427%	2.094%	1.806%	1.558%	1.344%	1.159%	1.000%		
66	2.500%	2.157%	1.860%	1.605%	1.384%	1.194%	1.030%		
67	2.575%	2.221%	1.916%	1.653%	1.426%	1.230%	1.061%		
68	2.652%	2.288%	1.974%	1.702%	1.469%	1.267%	1.093%		
69	2.732%	2.357%	2.033%	1.754%	1.513%	1.305%	1.126%		
70	2.814%	2.427%	2.094%	1.806%	1.558%	1.344%	1.159%	1.000%	
71	2.898%	2.500%	2.157%	1.860%	1.605%	1.384%	1.194%	1.030%	
72	2.985%	2.575%	2.221%	1.916%	1.653%	1.426%	1.230%	1.061%	
73	3.075%	2.652%	2.288%	1.974%	1.702%	1.469%	1.267%	1.093%	
74	3.167%	2.732%	2.357%	2.033%	1.754%	1.513%	1.305%	1.126%	
75	3.262%	2.814%	2.427%	2.094%	1.806%	1.558%	1.344%	1.159%	1.000%
76	3.360%	2.898%	2.500%	2.157%	1.860%	1.605%	1.384%	1.194%	1.030%
77	3.461%	2.985%	2.575%	2.221%	1.916%	1.653%	1.426%	1.230%	1.061%
78	3.565%	3.075%	2.652%	2.288%	1.974%	1.702%	1.469%	1.267%	1.093%
79	3.671%	3.167%	2.732%	2.357%	2.033%	1.754%	1.513%	1.305%	1.126%
80	3.782%	3.262%	2.814%	2.427%	2.094%	1.806%	1.558%	1.344%	1.159%
81	3.895%	3.360%	2.898%	2.500%	2.157%	1.860%	1.605%	1.384%	1.194%
82	4.012%	3.461%	2.985%	2.575%	2.221%	1.916%	1.653%	1.426%	1.230%
83	4.132%	3.565%	3.075%	2.652%	2.288%	1.974%	1.702%	1.469%	1.267%
84	4.256%	3.671%	3.167%	2.732%	2.357%	2.033%	1.754%	1.513%	1.305%
85	4.384%	3.782%	3.262%	2.814%	2.427%	2.094%	1.806%	1.558%	1.344%
86	4.515%	3.895%	3.360%	2.898%	2.500%	2.157%	1.860%	1.605%	1.384%
87	4.651%	4.012%	3.461%	2.985%	2.575%	2.221%	1.916%	1.653%	1.426%
88	4.790%	4.132%	3.565%	3.075%	2.652%	2.288%	1.974%	1.702%	1.469%
89	4.934%	4.256%	3.671%	3.167%	2.732%	2.357%	2.033%	1.754%	1.513%
90	5.082%	4.384%	3.782%	3.262%	2.814%	2.427%	2.094%	1.806%	1.558%
91	5.235%	4.515%	3.895%	3.360%	2.898%	2.500%	2.157%	1.860%	1.605%
92	5.392%	4.651%	4.012%	3.461%	2.985%	2.575%	2.221%	1.916%	1.653%
93	5.553%	4.790%	4.132%	3.565%	3.075%	2.652%	2.288%	1.974%	1.702%
94	5.720%	4.934%	4.256%	3.671%	3.167%	2.732%	2.357%	2.033%	1.754%

(*Continued*)

Flow	Current Age								
Year	35	40	45	50	55	60	65	70	75
95	5.892%	5.082%	4.384%	3.782%	3.262%	2.814%	2.427%	2.094%	1.806%
96	6.068%	5.235%	4.515%	3.895%	3.360%	2.898%	2.500%	2.157%	1.860%
97	6.250%	5.392%	4.651%	4.012%	3.461%	2.985%	2.575%	2.221%	1.916%
98	6.438%	5.553%	4.790%	4.132%	3.565%	3.075%	2.652%	2.288%	1.974%
99	6.631%	5.720%	4.934%	4.256%	3.671%	3.167%	2.732%	2.357%	2.033%
100	6.830%	5.892%	5.082%	4.384%	3.782%	3.262%	2.814%	2.427%	2.094%

8. We want to use actual prices where available and conservative values for prices where actual prices are unavailable. (In practice, I would use actual prices as far as I could. Then, for values further out, I would discount the last observed price at a low rate for which I had some comfort.) The most conservative approach would be to create a stack of payments at the furthest point that is executable and then move the matured stack to a cash account which would roll off as the remaining payments are made.

Flow	Current Age								
Year	35	40	45	50	55	60	65	70	75
65	0.231	0.295	0.377	0.481	0.614	0.784	1.000		
66	0.220	0.281	0.359	0.458	0.585	0.746	0.952		
67	0.210	0.268	0.342	0.436	0.557	0.711	0.907		
68	0.200	0.255	0.326	0.416	0.530	0.677	0.864		
69	0.190	0.243	0.310	0.396	0.505	0.645	0.823		
70	0.181	0.231	0.295	0.377	0.481	0.614	0.784	1.000	
71	0.173	0.220	0.281	0.359	0.458	0.585	0.746	0.952	
72	0.164	0.210	0.268	0.342	0.436	0.557	0.711	0.907	
73	0.157	0.200	0.255	0.326	0.416	0.530	0.677	0.864	
74	0.149	0.190	0.243	0.310	0.396	0.505	0.645	0.823	
75	0.142	0.181	0.231	0.295	0.377	0.481	0.614	0.784	1.000
76	0.135	0.173	0.220	0.281	0.359	0.458	0.585	0.746	0.952
77	0.129	0.164	0.210	0.268	0.342	0.436	0.557	0.711	0.907
78	0.123	0.157	0.200	0.255	0.326	0.416	0.530	0.677	0.864
79	0.117	0.149	0.190	0.243	0.310	0.396	0.505	0.645	0.823
80	0.111	0.142	0.181	0.231	0.295	0.377	0.481	0.614	0.784
81	0.106	0.135	0.173	0.220	0.281	0.359	0.458	0.585	0.746
82	0.101	0.129	0.164	0.210	0.268	0.342	0.436	0.557	0.711
83	0.096	0.123	0.157	0.200	0.255	0.326	0.416	0.530	0.677
84	0.092	0.117	0.149	0.190	0.243	0.310	0.396	0.505	0.645

Flow Year	Current Age								
	35	40	45	50	55	60	65	70	75
85	0.087	0.111	0.142	0.181	0.231	0.295	0.377	0.481	0.614
86	0.083	0.106	0.135	0.173	0.220	0.281	0.359	0.458	0.585
87	0.079	0.101	0.129	0.164	0.210	0.268	0.342	0.436	0.557
88	0.075	0.096	0.123	0.157	0.200	0.255	0.326	0.416	0.530
89	0.072	0.092	0.117	0.149	0.190	0.243	0.310	0.396	0.505
90	0.068	0.087	0.111	0.142	0.181	0.231	0.295	0.377	0.481
91	0.065	0.083	0.106	0.135	0.173	0.220	0.281	0.359	0.458
92	0.062	0.079	0.101	0.129	0.164	0.210	0.268	0.342	0.436
93	0.059	0.075	0.096	0.123	0.157	0.200	0.255	0.326	0.416
94	0.056	0.072	0.092	0.117	0.149	0.190	0.243	0.310	0.396
95	0.054	0.068	0.087	0.111	0.142	0.181	0.231	0.295	0.377
96	0.051	0.065	0.083	0.106	0.135	0.173	0.220	0.281	0.359
97	0.049	0.062	0.079	0.101	0.129	0.164	0.210	0.268	0.342
98	0.046	0.059	0.075	0.096	0.123	0.157	0.200	0.255	0.326
99	0.044	0.056	0.072	0.092	0.117	0.149	0.190	0.243	0.310
100	0.042	0.054	0.068	0.087	0.111	0.142	0.181	0.231	0.295

9. Once we multiply the elements of the tables from Problems 7 and 8, we are one step away from creating a usable flooring allocation.

Flow Year	Current Age								
	35	40	45	50	55	60	65	70	75
65	0.006	0.006	0.007	0.007	0.008	0.009	0.010		
66	0.006	0.006	0.007	0.007	0.008	0.009	0.010		
67	0.005	0.006	0.007	0.007	0.008	0.009	0.010		
68	0.005	0.006	0.006	0.007	0.008	0.009	0.009		
69	0.005	0.006	0.006	0.007	0.008	0.008	0.009		
70	0.005	0.006	0.006	0.007	0.007	0.008	0.009	0.010	
71	0.005	0.006	0.006	0.007	0.007	0.008	0.009	0.010	
72	0.005	0.005	0.006	0.007	0.007	0.008	0.009	0.010	
73	0.005	0.005	0.006	0.006	0.007	0.008	0.009	0.009	
74	0.005	0.005	0.006	0.006	0.007	0.008	0.008	0.009	
75	0.005	0.005	0.006	0.006	0.007	0.007	0.008	0.009	0.010
76	0.005	0.005	0.006	0.006	0.007	0.007	0.008	0.009	0.010
77	0.004	0.005	0.005	0.006	0.007	0.007	0.008	0.009	0.010
78	0.004	0.005	0.005	0.006	0.006	0.007	0.008	0.009	0.009
79	0.004	0.005	0.005	0.006	0.006	0.007	0.008	0.008	0.009
80	0.004	0.005	0.005	0.006	0.006	0.007	0.007	0.008	0.009

(*Continued*)

Flow	Current Age								
Year	35	40	45	50	55	60	65	70	75
81	0.004	0.005	0.005	0.006	0.006	0.007	0.007	0.008	0.009
82	0.004	0.004	0.005	0.005	0.006	0.007	0.007	0.008	0.009
83	0.004	0.004	0.005	0.005	0.006	0.006	0.007	0.008	0.009
84	0.004	0.004	0.005	0.005	0.006	0.006	0.007	0.008	0.008
85	0.004	0.004	0.005	0.005	0.006	0.006	0.007	0.007	0.008
86	0.004	0.004	0.005	0.005	0.006	0.006	0.007	0.007	0.008
87	0.004	0.004	0.004	0.005	0.005	0.006	0.007	0.007	0.008
88	0.004	0.004	0.004	0.005	0.005	0.006	0.006	0.007	0.008
89	0.004	0.004	0.004	0.005	0.005	0.006	0.006	0.007	0.008
90	0.003	0.004	0.004	0.005	0.005	0.006	0.006	0.007	0.007
91	0.003	0.004	0.004	0.005	0.005	0.006	0.006	0.007	0.007
92	0.003	0.004	0.004	0.004	0.005	0.005	0.006	0.007	0.007
93	0.003	0.004	0.004	0.004	0.005	0.005	0.006	0.006	0.007
94	0.003	0.004	0.004	0.004	0.005	0.005	0.006	0.006	0.007
95	0.003	0.003	0.004	0.004	0.005	0.005	0.006	0.006	0.007
96	0.003	0.003	0.004	0.004	0.005	0.005	0.006	0.006	0.007
97	0.003	0.003	0.004	0.004	0.004	0.005	0.005	0.006	0.007
98	0.003	0.003	0.004	0.004	0.004	0.005	0.005	0.006	0.006
99	0.003	0.003	0.004	0.004	0.004	0.005	0.005	0.006	0.006
100	0.003	0.003	0.003	0.004	0.004	0.005	0.005	0.006	0.006

10. Creating flooring at 1 percent of current wealth with $g = 3\%$ and $r = 5\%$ beginning at age 65 can be found in the next table.

	Current Age					
	35	40	45	50	55	60
Sum to 80	7.8%	8.6%	9.5%	10.4%	11.5%	12.6%
Sum to 85	9.8%	10.8%	11.9%	13.1%	14.4%	15.8%
Sum to 90	11.6%	12.8%	14.1%	15.5%	17.0%	18.8%
Sum to 95	13.2%	14.6%	16.0%	17.7%	19.5%	21.4%
Sum to 100	14.7%	16.2%	17.9%	19.7%	21.6%	23.8%

11. Using the technology that you created in Problems 7–10, finding the flooring allocation required for a 45 year old to create a floor at 5 percent of his current financial wealth given yields of 4 percent and a growth rate for the payment stream of 1 percent is 44.32 percent:

$$\text{Pct of Wealth} \times \sum_i (1+g)^i \times \text{Strip cost}_i = 5\% \times \sum_{i=20}^{40} \left(\frac{1.01}{1.04}\right)^i$$

Keep in mind that in real applications the prices of the payments will be observed from market data rather than calculated by using an assumed constant rate.

12. We construct the tables for longevity to cover out to age 105. While not a physical limit, it is the practical limit for most of our clients. You may have tables that extend to any age. For clarity, we show a fragment of the table.

	Current Age					
	35	40	45	50	55	60
sum(81-105)	0.047	0.054	0.069	0.085	0.084	0.097
sum(86-105)	0.035	0.040	0.053	0.066	0.062	0.072
sum(91-105)	0.024	0.028	0.039	0.050	0.043	0.050
sum(96-105)	0.015	0.017	0.026	0.035	0.026	0.031
sum(101-105)	0.007	0.008	0.016	0.023	0.012	0.014

13. If the general payment stream is given by Pct of Wealth $\times$

$$\sum_{i=20}^{40} \Pr(\text{Survival to pmt}_i | \text{Alive}_{i-1}) \Pr(\text{Alive}_{i-1})(1+g)^i \times \text{PV}_i \text{ then in our}$$

particular case, where the probability of survival to the age when the cash flows begin is 40 percent; and if survival at the start of the payments guarantees receipt of all payments, then the 45-year-old client will need to allocate 13.22 percent to longevity protection.

14. The allocations for this particular client work out to:

Flooring: 44%

Longevity: 13%

Precautionary: 5%

At risk: 38%

15. For a 50-year-old client, inflation 2 percent, rates 6 percent, floored at 4 percent of wealth, and longevity insurance to be purchased to begin paying at age 90, the allocations are as follows:

Flooring: 38%

Longevity: 4%

Precautionary: 5%

At risk: 53%

To accomplish the transition in this case is relatively straightforward and only requires small changes in the current portfolio. The fixed income allocation of 30 percent can be translated pretty easily into flooring. The equity allocation will only need to be reduced by 7 percent (but there is a possibility of a change in the desired level of risk once flooring is secured). The remainder of the needs can be met by using the excess precautionary balances of 10 percent and using about half of the amount to take precaution against an impoverished longevity.

16. Even if the client only wants to create flooring out to age 80, the combination of late-stage planning (age 65), high draw rate 7 percent, and high inflation relative to discount rates make capital market solutions infeasible. This client will need to consider some of the following options:
    - Monetize mortality
    - Delay retirement
    - Only partially retire
    - Reduce lifestyle

17. For a 45-year-old client who wants to create a floor at 4 percent of current assets, assuming a 2 percent rate of anticipated inflation and a 6 percent yield curve, the flooring allocations will be the following:

Age	Flooring Allocation Per 1 Percent	Total Flooring Allocation
45	8%	31%
46	8%	32%
47	8%	34%
48	9%	35%
49	9%	36%
50	9%	38%
51	10%	39%
52	10%	41%
53	11%	42%
54	11%	44%
55	11%	46%
56	12%	47%
57	12%	49%
58	13%	51%
59	13%	53%
60	14%	55%
61	14%	57%
62	15%	60%
63	16%	62%
64	16%	64%
65	17%	67%

18. For an underfunded client, annuitization may be the only feasible way for her to maintain lifestyle without deferring retirement or reevaluating lifestyle needs. If the amount by which the client is underfunded is small, then (just as with an overfunded client) she may find an annuity to be an attractive method for creating enough slack for a meaningful upside portfolio to exist alongside the flooring. If the amount by which the client is underfunded is extreme, then there is little chance for upside.

The saving grace for this client is age. She may be underfunded or on a trajectory that implies an underfunded state in the future. With a full assessment of the gap and a thoughtful and feasible plan for closing the gap, this client may be willing and able to alter the current trajectory.

CHAPTER 8

Rebalancing Retirement Income Portfolios

1. Without rebalancing, the portfolio will decline to $777,000:

Period	Beginning Equity	Equity Return	Beginning Fixed Income	Fixed Income Return	Ending Portfolio
1	$600,000	–20%	$400,000	5%	$900,000
2	$480,000	–30%	$420,000	5%	$777,000

2. With rebalancing, the portfolio fares worse in a consecutively down market:

Period	Beginning Equity	Equity Return	Beginning Fixed Income	Fixed Income Return	Ending Portfolio
1	$600,000	–20%	$400,000	5%	$900,000
2	$540,000	–30%	$360,000	5%	$756,000

3. In accumulation without rebalancing, the portfolio grows to nearly $3.6 million.

Period	Beginning Equity	Equity Return	Beginning Fixed Income	Fixed Income Return	Ending Portfolio
1	$600,000	–20%	$400,000	5%	$900,000
2	$506,667	–45%	$443,333	5%	$744,167
3	$297,390	5%	$496,777	5%	$833,875
4	$330,983	7%	$552,892	5%	$934,688
5	$373,097	–11%	$611,592	5%	$974,227
6	$349,098	–10%	$675,129	5%	$1,023,074
7	$329,543	10%	$743,531	5%	$1,143,205
8	$378,352	8%	$814,853	5%	$1,264,216
9	$424,781	–10%	$889,434	5%	$1,316,209

(*Continued*)

Period	Beginning Equity	Equity Return	Beginning Fixed Income	Fixed Income Return	Ending Portfolio
10	$396,826	7%	$969,383	5%	$1,442,456
11	$439,322	–10%	$1,053,134	5%	$1,501,181
12	$408,559	–10%	$1,142,622	5%	$1,567,456
13	$379,433	10%	$1,238,023	5%	$1,717,300
14	$429,528	30%	$1,337,772	5%	$1,963,047
15	$572,609	5%	$1,440,439	5%	$2,113,700
16	$615,462	10%	$1,548,238	5%	$2,302,658
17	$691,708	30%	$1,660,950	5%	$2,643,218
18	$916,231	7%	$1,776,987	5%	$2,846,203
19	$997,589	30%	$1,898,614	5%	$3,290,411
20	$1,316,573	10%	$2,023,838	5%	$3,573,260

4. In accumulation with rebalancing, the portfolio grows to over $3.8 million.

Period	Beginning Equity	Equity Return	Beginning Fixed Income	Fixed Income Return	Ending Portfolio
1	$600,000	–20%	$400,000	5%	$900,000
2	$570,000	–45%	$380,000	5%	$712,500
3	$457,500	5%	$305,000	5%	$800,625
4	$510,375	7%	$340,250	5%	$903,364
5	$572,018	–11%	$381,346	5%	$909,509
6	$575,705	–10%	$383,804	5%	$921,129
7	$582,677	10%	$388,451	5%	$1,048,819
8	$659,291	8%	$439,528	5%	$1,173,539
9	$734,123	–10%	$489,415	5%	$1,174,597
10	$734,758	7%	$489,839	5%	$1,300,522
11	$810,313	–10%	$540,209	5%	$1,296,501
12	$807,901	–10%	$538,600	5%	$1,292,641
13	$805,585	10%	$537,056	5%	$1,450,052
14	$900,031	30%	$600,021	5%	$1,800,063
15	$1,110,038	5%	$740,025	5%	$1,942,566
16	$1,195,540	10%	$797,026	5%	$2,151,971
17	$1,321,183	30%	$880,789	5%	$2,642,366
18	$1,615,419	7%	$1,076,946	5%	$2,859,292
19	$1,745,575	30%	$1,163,717	5%	$3,491,151
20	$2,124,690	10%	$1,416,460	5%	$3,824,443

Clearly during a period that has net positive drift, rebalancing achieves a higher total portfolio value. However, the result is not necessarily true if the drift is not positive: Consider the Japanese experience from 1979–2009. You can also show yourself that for accumulation—a sawtooth pattern –10, +10, –10, +10 ...—the dollar-cost-averaging impact of rebalancing is beneficial even if the market goes nowhere.

5. Without rebalancing, the portfolio fails after 19 periods:

Period	Beginning Equity	Equity Return	Beginning Fixed Income	Fixed Income Return	Ending Portfolio
1	$600,000	–20%	$400,000	5%	$900,000
2	$453,333	–45%	$396,667	5%	$665,833
3	$230,610	5%	$385,223	5%	$646,625
4	$223,417	7%	$373,208	5%	$630,925
5	$220,111	–11%	$360,813	5%	$574,753
6	$178,857	–10%	$345,896	5%	$524,162
7	$145,616	10%	$328,546	5%	$505,151
8	$144,323	8%	$310,828	5%	$482,238
9	$139,708	–10%	$292,530	5%	$432,894
10	$111,215	7%	$271,679	5%	$404,263
11	$104,281	–10%	$249,981	5%	$356,334
12	$80,684	–10%	$225,650	5%	$309,548
13	$60,886	10%	$198,662	5%	$275,570
14	$54,823	30%	$170,747	5%	$250,554
15	$57,047	5%	$143,507	5%	$210,582
16	$45,677	10%	$114,904	5%	$170,895
17	$35,544	30%	$85,350	5%	$135,825
18	$29,198	7%	$56,628	5%	$90,701
19	$14,019	30%	$26,681	5%	$46,240

Failure occurs as soon as the ending value of the portfolio is less than the withdrawal needed for that period.

6. With rebalancing, the portfolio fails sooner, even though the net drift of the portfolio over the full 20 periods is positive:

Period	Beginning Equity	Equity Return	Beginning Fixed Income	Fixed Income Return	Ending Portfolio
1	$600,000	–20%	$400,000	5%	$900,000
2	$510,000	–45%	$340,000	5%	$637,500
3	$352,500	5%	$235,000	5%	$616,875
4	$340,125	7%	$226,750	5%	$602,021

(*Continued*)

Period	Beginning Equity	Equity Return	Beginning Fixed Income	Fixed Income Return	Ending Portfolio
5	$331,213	–11%	$220,809	5%	$526,628
6	$285,977	–10%	$190,651	5%	$457,563
7	$244,538	10%	$163,025	5%	$440,168
8	$234,101	8%	$156,067	5%	$416,700
9	$220,020	–10%	$146,680	5%	$352,032
10	$181,219	7%	$120,813	5%	$320,758
11	$162,455	–10%	$108,303	5%	$259,927
12	$125,956	–10%	$83,971	5%	$201,530
13	$90,918	10%	$60,612	5%	$163,653
14	$68,192	30%	$45,461	5%	$136,383
15	$51,830	5%	$34,553	5%	$90,702
16	$24,421	10%	$16,281	5%	$43,958

7. Creating nominal dollar flooring at 6 percent of wealth designed to pay out from ages 66 through 89 with a 6 percent yield curve implies the following allocation schedule:

Age	Flooring Allocation Per 1%	Total Flooring Allocation
40	3%	18%
41	3%	19%
42	3%	20%
43	3%	21%
44	4%	22%
45	4%	23%
46	4%	25%
47	4%	26%
48	5%	28%
49	5%	30%
50	5%	31%
51	6%	33%
52	6%	35%
53	6%	37%
54	7%	40%
55	7%	42%
56	7%	45%
57	8%	47%
58	8%	50%
59	9%	53%

8. Assuming the returns shown and annual rebalancing back to target, the client's portfolio follows this path:

Age	Beginning Risky Portfolio	Risky Portfolio Return	Beginning Flooring	Flooring Accretion	Ending Portfolio
40	$824,547	−0.048%	$175,453	5%	$1,008,380
41	$820,842	0.510%	$187,539	5%	$1,021,947
42	$820,481	18.579%	$201,466	5%	$1,184,460
43	$936,947	−13.918%	$247,513	5%	$1,066,429
44	$830,209	−11.050%	$236,220	5%	$986,502
45	$754,876	3.428%	$231,626	5%	$1,023,961
46	$769,114	17.559%	$254,847	5%	$1,171,755
47	$862,627	5.403%	$309,128	5%	$1,233,820
48	$888,788	19.584%	$345,032	5%	$1,425,127
49	$1,002,685	16.246%	$422,442	5%	$1,609,144
50	$1,103,536	20.510%	$505,608	5%	$1,860,765
51	$1,241,014	−13.515%	$619,750	5%	$1,724,033
52	$1,115,370	−14.589%	$608,663	5%	$1,591,740
53	$996,066	19.673%	$595,675	5%	$1,817,477
54	$1,096,516	33.834%	$720,961	5%	$2,224,518
55	$1,289,146	16.101%	$935,373	5%	$2,478,851
56	$1,373,997	−6.741%	$1,104,854	5%	$2,441,473
57	$1,287,987	18.290%	$1,153,486	5%	$2,734,718
58	$1,365,165	16.305%	$1,369,553	5%	$3,025,790
59	$1,419,548	−8.174%	$1,606,242	5%	$2,990,062

Notice that instead of a fixed-income component and fixed income, we have columns for flooring and accretion of the flooring. Similarly, we have risky portfolio amount and risky portfolio returns. Notice also that with two-sided rebalancing (rebalance both in up and down markets), we end up with the undesirable result that the flooring can decrease in down markets. (See, for example, the changes in flooring from age 43 to 44, 44 to 45, 52 to 53, and again from 54 to 55.) You may want to set up your own return stream: Most standard spreadsheet applications allow you to create streams of random numbers.

9. To set up this solution, you need to create the one-sided allocation schedule: If the portfolio hits a new high then rebalance to target allocations, otherwise the flooring allocation will be the accreted value of the previous period's flooring relative to the portfolio value.

A comparison of the flooring allocations under two-sided versus one-sided rebalancing can be seen next:

Age	Total Flooring Allocation	One-Sided Rebalancing Flooring Allocation
40	17.55%	17.55%
41	18.60%	18.60%
42	19.71%	19.71%
43	20.90%	20.90%
44	22.15%	24.37%
45	23.48%	27.56%
46	24.89%	27.86%
47	26.38%	25.64%
48	27.96%	27.96%
49	29.64%	29.64%
50	31.42%	31.42%
51	33.31%	33.31%
52	35.30%	37.75%
53	37.42%	42.71%
54	39.67%	39.54%
55	42.05%	42.05%
56	44.57%	44.57%
57	47.25%	47.52%
58	50.08%	50.08%
59	53.09%	53.09%

Notice that in the down equity states the flooring allocation is allowed to rise above the target allocations. The resulting portfolio dollar allocations and total portfolio values are given by the following table:

Age	Beginning Risky Portfolio	Risky Portfolio Return	Beginning Flooring	Flooring Accretion	Ending Portfolio
40	$824,547	0%	$175,453	5%	$1,008,380
41	$820,842	1%	$187,539	5%	$1,021,947
42	$820,481	19%	$201,466	5%	$1,184,460
43	$936,947	−14%	$247,513	5%	$1,066,429
44	$806,539	−11%	$259,889	5%	$990,301
45	$717,418	3%	$272,884	5%	$1,028,538
46	$742,011	18%	$286,528	5%	$1,173,157
47	$872,303	5%	$300,854	5%	$1,235,332

Age	Beginning Risky Portfolio	Risky Portfolio Return	Beginning Flooring	Flooring Accretion	Ending Portfolio
48	$889,877	20%	$345,455	5%	$1,426,873
49	$1,003,914	16%	$422,960	5%	$1,611,116
50	$1,104,888	21%	$506,228	5%	$1,863,045
51	$1,242,535	−14%	$620,510	5%	$1,726,145
52	$1,074,610	−15%	$651,535	5%	$1,601,943
53	$917,831	20%	$684,112	5%	$1,816,711
54	$1,098,393	34%	$718,317	5%	$2,224,255
55	$1,288,993	16%	$935,262	5%	$2,478,558
56	$1,373,834	−7%	$1,104,724	5%	$2,441,184
57	$1,281,224	18%	$1,159,960	5%	$2,733,516
58	$1,364,565	16%	$1,368,951	5%	$3,024,460
59	$1,418,924	−8%	$1,605,536	5%	$2,988,748

Notice also, that one-sided rebalancing has a cost (that is small as an artifact of this particular example) in terms of a lower final portfolio value. Before the fact, one never knows with certainty whether the one-sided rebalancing will impose a cost or save the client from disaster, but it takes the disaster scenarios off the table and raises the amount of flooring in those periods when rebalancing *toward* flooring occurs.

10. The problem started with flooring of $60,000 per year running from age 66 to 90. Had we not rebalanced, the flooring would have risen in value from $175,453 to $465,529. By using one-sided rebalancing and adding to flooring when risky allocations performed well, we end up the process with $1,605,536 in flooring, about 3.45 × the original amount, that is, $206,931 per year.

The cost of flooring is also changing over the rebalancing interval. It may be changing due to interest-rate fluctuations; and it will definitely be changing due to the pull to par of shorter maturity. The best choice, though ruled out by the client, is to be prepared to rebalance more frequently. Alternatively, it is reasonable to add a couple of percents to the calculated floor to cover accretion of the floor over the rebalancing period, plus the potential impact of interest rate volatility. In other words, estimate the cushion based on the next rebalancing period's potential cost of flooring.

CHAPTER 9

Active Risk Management for Retirement Income Portfolios

1. In a steadily rising market, one-sided rebalancing imposes no cost on the portfolio. The greatest costs from engaging in risk management will occur in volatile markets where declines lead to rebounds.

2. Whipsaw markets would tend to favor simple one-sided rebalancing since the up years would be more likely to allow for capture of additional flooring. Persistence would tend to favor high-water rebalancing since it would allow for the risky portfolio to take advantage of some market momentum before rebalancing toward flooring. The danger for high-water flooring is that in a whipsaw market flooring would be less likely to be incremented before the next down move in the portfolio. In persistent markets, incrementing flooring at high frequency decreases the value of momentum.

3. For this client the total cost of flooring is $994,215. With a total portfolio value of $1,500,000, the cushion is $505,785:

Maturity in Years	Price	$80,000 Flooring Cost
1	$99.04	
2	$96.87	
3	$94.54	
4	$90.28	
5	$86.49	$69,195
6	$83.40	$66,720
7	$76.94	$61,554
8	$73.00	$58,397
9	$69.79	$55,832
10	$65.74	$52,590
11	$60.36	$48,287
12	$57.05	$45,640

(*Continued*)

Maturity in Years	Price	$80,000 Flooring Cost
13	$54.04	$43,231
14	$51.23	$40,987
15	$48.96	$39,168
16	$46.91	$37,525
17	$45.38	$36,303
18	$42.68	$34,146
19	$41.16	$32,929
20	$39.60	$31,683
21	$38.28	$30,626
22	$36.59	$29,270
23	$35.56	$28,445
24	$34.40	$27,516
25	$33.11	$26,486
26	$31.83	$25,464
27	$30.63	$24,505
28	$30.18	$24,145
29	$29.46	$23,570
30	$28.78	
	Total Flooring Cost	$994,215
	Portfolio Value	$1,500,000
	Cushion	$505,785

4. With a multiplier of 2, the allocations for the relevant part of the table (data-linked live spreadsheet?) would be as follows:

Maturity in Years	Price	$80,000 Flooring Cost
	Total Cost	$994,215
	Portfolio	$1,500,000
	Cushion	$505,785
	Multiplier	2.00
	Target Risky Allocation	$1,011,569
	Target Floor Allocation	$488,431

Note that by adding in a couple of rows for (live data feed of) actual values of the risky portfolio and flooring, one can create an operational spreadsheet that can be managed by an assistant. Furthermore, several hundred clients can be managed on a single spreadsheet. Although our answers to subsequent problems in this chapter will show tables, the presentation here is closer to what you will need to see in practice in order to manage client portfolios. (In the following answers, we want to show what happens to a single portfolio through time.)

5. If the portfolio is only going to be rebalanced periodically, then you may need to adjust the cushion to take into account the cost of flooring at the time of rebalancing. This is particularly true if the cushion is low and there is the possibility that a decline in rates may completely wipe out the cushion. If rates were fixed, then the task would be trivial. But since there is volatility in rates, you need to factor in an adjustment for the possibility that rates may decline between rebalancing dates.

6a. The cumulative return for the data in the table is 14 percent for the risky portfolio and 26 percent for the cost of flooring.

6b. In a case like this, increasing exposure to risky assets with active risk management underperforms a static portfolio. Before the fact, you never know what the roll of the dice will bring. In this case, the flooring costs rise faster, on average, than the risky portfolio.

7. This approach is equivalent to a working with a multiplier of 1. Starting with an initial portfolio value of $1,500,000 yields, you get the following evolution:

Quarter	Cost of Flooring	Cushion	Risky Allocation	Flooring Allocation	Ending Portfolio Value
1	$994,215	$505,785	$505,785	$994,215	$1,516,552
2	$1,002,169	$514,383	$514,383	$1,002,169	$1,551,446
3	$1,013,093	$538,353	$538,353	$1,013,093	$1,543,124
4	$1,023,021	$520,103	$520,103	$1,023,021	$1,585,185
5	$1,033,251	$551,933	$551,933	$1,033,251	$1,539,939
6	$1,042,757	$497,182	$497,182	$1,042,757	$1,586,000
7	$1,052,872	$533,128	$533,128	$1,052,872	$1,601,279
8	$1,062,979	$538,299	$538,299	$1,062,979	$1,621,812
9	$1,073,716	$548,096	$548,096	$1,073,716	$1,615,601
10	$1,082,413	$533,188	$533,188	$1,082,413	$1,628,343
11	$1,093,129	$535,214	$535,214	$1,093,129	$1,633,930
12	$1,101,874	$532,056	$532,056	$1,101,874	$1,659,155
13	$1,112,892	$546,262	$546,262	$1,112,892	$1,616,998
14	$1,122,686	$494,313	$494,313	$1,122,686	$1,638,241
15	$1,135,821	$502,419	$502,419	$1,135,821	$1,602,282
16	$1,149,451	$452,831	$452,831	$1,149,451	$1,622,902
17	$1,161,060	$461,842	$461,842	$1,161,060	$1,608,176
18	$1,170,581	$437,595	$437,595	$1,170,581	$1,673,633
19	$1,182,170	$491,463	$491,463	$1,182,170	$1,753,699
20	$1,193,873	$559,826	$559,826	$1,193,873	$1,782,485

(*Continued*)

Quarter	Cost of Flooring	Cushion	Risky Allocation	Flooring Allocation	Ending Portfolio Value
21	$1,206,648	$575,837	$575,837	$1,206,648	$1,744,862
22	$1,218,835	$526,027	$526,027	$1,218,835	$1,764,007
23	$1,229,195	$534,812	$534,812	$1,229,195	$1,782,300
24	$1,240,750	$541,550	$541,550	$1,240,750	$1,829,637

In practice, one would want to make sure that the ending portfolio values were net of fees for management (usually certain) or if transaction based, rebalancing costs (usually estimable).

8. For a multiplier of 2, and using these unlucky data, the portfolio evolution underperforms the lower multiplier evolution:

Quarter	Cost of Flooring	Cushion	Risky Allocation	Flooring Allocation	Ending Portfolio Value
1	$994,215	$505,785	$1,011,569	$488,431	$1,521,104
2	$1,002,169	$518,935	$1,037,870	$483,234	$1,574,736
3	$1,013,093	$561,643	$1,123,287	$451,449	$1,541,081
4	$1,023,021	$518,060	$1,036,120	$504,961	$1,609,541
5	$1,033,251	$576,290	$1,152,580	$456,961	$1,499,409
6	$1,042,757	$456,652	$913,304	$586,105	$1,571,126
7	$1,052,872	$518,254	$1,036,509	$534,617	$1,586,313
8	$1,062,979	$523,333	$1,046,667	$539,646	$1,610,813
9	$1,073,716	$537,097	$1,074,194	$536,619	$1,585,941
10	$1,082,413	$503,528	$1,007,057	$578,884	$1,595,499
11	$1,093,129	$502,370	$1,004,741	$590,758	$1,594,297
12	$1,101,874	$492,423	$984,847	$609,450	$1,626,687
13	$1,112,892	$513,795	$1,027,589	$599,098	$1,534,235
14	$1,122,686	$411,549	$823,099	$711,136	$1,556,054
15	$1,135,821	$420,233	$840,466	$715,588	$1,481,687
16	$1,149,451	$332,236	$664,473	$817,215	$1,503,164
17	$1,161,060	$342,104	$684,207	$818,957	$1,473,959
18	$1,170,581	$303,378	$606,755	$867,204	$1,557,236
19	$1,182,170	$375,066	$750,131	$807,104	$1,669,569
20	$1,193,873	$475,696	$951,392	$718,178	$1,704,464
21	$1,206,648	$497,816	$995,631	$708,832	$1,625,501
22	$1,218,835	$406,666	$813,331	$812,169	$1,645,987
23	$1,229,195	$416,792	$833,583	$812,403	$1,664,126
24	$1,240,750	$423,377	$846,754	$817,373	$1,726,916

Note: Hopefully you constructed this in a spreadsheet and can play around with the multiplier. In general, you want to add in a couple of constraints on leverage. The first constraint to add is to ensure that the risky allocation is not allowed to exceed the portfolio value—that is, no leverage. You also want to ensure that the flooring allocation isn't allowed to become negative. It is possible that a crash between rebalancing dates can force the cushion negative, so it is important to keep the option open to rebalance at intermediate dates under extreme circumstances: The goal is to protect the floor and seek upside, not just one or the other.

9. With the new data and a multiplier of 1, the portfolio evolves as follows:

Quarter	Cost of Flooring	Cushion	Risky Allocation	Flooring Allocation	Ending Portfolio Value
1	$994,215	$505,785	$505,785	$994,215	$1,522,874
2	$1,002,169	$520,705	$520,705	$1,002,169	$1,564,572
3	$1,013,093	$551,479	$551,479	$1,013,093	$1,562,698
4	$1,023,021	$539,677	$539,677	$1,023,021	$1,612,703
5	$1,033,251	$579,452	$579,452	$1,033,251	$1,571,970
6	$1,042,757	$529,213	$529,213	$1,042,757	$1,626,962
7	$1,052,872	$574,090	$574,090	$1,052,872	$1,649,815
8	$1,062,979	$586,835	$586,835	$1,062,979	$1,678,567
9	$1,073,716	$604,851	$604,851	$1,073,716	$1,678,372
10	$1,082,413	$595,960	$595,960	$1,082,413	$1,698,802
11	$1,093,129	$605,674	$605,674	$1,093,129	$1,711,545
12	$1,101,874	$609,671	$609,671	$1,101,874	$1,746,463
13	$1,112,892	$633,570	$633,570	$1,112,892	$1,703,923
14	$1,122,686	$581,238	$581,238	$1,122,686	$1,733,856
15	$1,135,821	$598,035	$598,035	$1,135,821	$1,695,936
16	$1,149,451	$546,485	$546,485	$1,149,451	$1,725,251
17	$1,161,060	$564,191	$564,191	$1,161,060	$1,712,204
18	$1,170,581	$541,623	$541,623	$1,170,581	$1,797,237
19	$1,182,170	$615,067	$615,067	$1,182,170	$1,902,185
20	$1,193,873	$708,311	$708,311	$1,193,873	$1,944,071
21	$1,206,648	$737,423	$737,423	$1,206,648	$1,901,689
22	$1,218,835	$682,854	$682,854	$1,218,835	$1,931,988
23	$1,229,195	$702,793	$702,793	$1,229,195	$1,961,183
24	$1,240,750	$720,433	$720,433	$1,240,750	$2,029,063

10. With a multiplier of 2, the evolution of the portfolio values is:

Quarter	Cost of Flooring	Cushion	Risky Allocation	Flooring Allocation	Ending Portfolio Value
1	$994,215	$505,785	$1,011,569	$488,431	$1,533,749
2	$1,002,169	$531,580	$1,063,159	$470,589	$1,601,711
3	$1,013,093	$588,618	$1,177,236	$424,475	$1,580,678
4	$1,023,021	$557,657	$1,115,314	$465,364	$1,667,530
5	$1,033,251	$634,279	$1,268,558	$398,972	$1,561,217
6	$1,042,757	$518,460	$1,036,919	$524,298	$1,654,233
7	$1,052,872	$601,361	$1,202,723	$451,511	$1,685,268
8	$1,062,979	$622,289	$1,244,577	$440,691	$1,727,928
9	$1,073,716	$654,212	$1,308,424	$419,503	$1,712,092
10	$1,082,413	$629,679	$1,259,358	$452,734	$1,737,101
11	$1,093,129	$643,973	$1,287,946	$449,156	$1,749,195
12	$1,101,874	$647,321	$1,294,643	$454,552	$1,804,491
13	$1,112,892	$691,598	$1,383,197	$421,294	$1,693,946
14	$1,122,686	$571,260	$1,142,520	$551,426	$1,733,416
15	$1,135,821	$597,595	$1,195,191	$538,226	$1,636,850
16	$1,149,451	$487,399	$974,797	$662,052	$1,675,120
17	$1,161,060	$514,059	$1,028,119	$647,001	$1,639,301
18	$1,170,581	$468,719	$937,439	$701,862	$1,773,366
19	$1,182,170	$591,196	$1,182,391	$590,974	$1,958,467
20	$1,193,873	$764,593	$1,529,187	$429,280	$2,025,910
21	$1,206,648	$819,262	$1,638,524	$387,386	$1,908,572
22	$1,218,835	$689,737	$1,379,473	$529,098	$1,953,350
23	$1,229,195	$724,154	$1,448,309	$505,041	$1,994,449
24	$1,240,750	$753,700	$1,507,400	$487,050	$2,115,390

As the multiplier is increased, the portfolio moves closer to being 100 percent invested in risky assets which is favorable in a rising market, unless the cushion is eliminated in a correction. Even though these are "lucky" data, the ending result with a multiplier of 4 is reduced to $2,019,383.

11. We now add a *ratchet* feature to our floor. To place a ratchet into our working model, if Cushion × Multiplier ≥ Portfolio value, then the portfolio will be 100 percent invested in the risky portfolio. So what

we want to do is take the excess, that is, Cushion × Multiplier – Portfolio value, placing the excess into the "cost of flooring" column and allocating percentagewise to the notional flooring pattern. We raise the multiplier to 3 in this problem to force a case where the ratchet operates given the client's proximity to retirement. The risky exposures are substantially below 100 percent unless we goose up the multiplier—something I do not suggest in practice. Remember, with a high multiplier, a quarter like autumn 2008 can wipe out the upside potential.

In the table that follows, I suppress the flooring allocation column to display the excess cushion:

Quarter	Cost of Flooring	Cushion	Excess Cushion	Risky Allocation	Ending Portfolio Value
1	$994,215	$505,785	$17,354	$1,500,000	$1,544,250
2	$1,019,662	$542,081	$81,993	$1,544,250	$1,635,515
3	$1,030,776	$604,739	$178,702	$1,635,515	$1,600,515
4	$1,040,878	$559,637	$78,397	$1,600,515	$1,718,473
5	$1,051,287	$667,187	$283,086	$1,718,473	$1,569,481
6	$1,060,958	$508,523	$—	$1,525,569	$1,699,276
7	$1,071,250	$628,026	$184,802	$1,699,276	$1,737,000
8	$1,081,534	$655,466	$229,398	$1,737,000	$1,790,326
9	$1,092,457	$697,868	$303,279	$1,790,326	$1,764,008
10	$1,101,306	$662,702	$224,097	$1,764,008	$1,792,761
11	$1,112,209	$680,552	$248,895	$1,792,761	$1,804,593
12	$1,121,107	$683,487	$245,866	$1,804,593	$1,875,333
13	$1,132,318	$743,016	$353,713	$1,875,333	$1,720,431
14	$1,142,282	$578,149	$14,015	$1,720,431	$1,770,151
15	$1,155,647	$614,504	$73,362	$1,770,151	$1,617,564
16	$1,169,515	$448,050	$—	$1,344,149	$1,663,876
17	$1,181,327	$482,549	$—	$1,447,648	$1,607,743
18	$1,191,014	$416,730	$—	$1,250,189	$1,780,809
19	$1,202,805	$578,004	$—	$1,734,012	$2,044,148
20	$1,214,712	$829,436	$444,159	$2,044,148	$2,128,163
21	$1,227,710	$900,453	$573,196	$2,128,163	$1,970,679
22	$1,240,110	$730,569	$221,028	$1,970,679	$2,028,222
23	$1,250,651	$777,572	$304,493	$2,028,222	$2,079,131
24	$1,262,407	$816,724	$371,041	$2,079,131	$2,239,224

12. We add a column for the payments to the client. Note that the flooring that rolls off does so at its notional value; it has matured.

Quarter	Cost of Flooring	Cushion	Risky Allocation	Ending Portfolio Value	Payment to Client
1	$994,215	$505,785	$1,011,569	$1,533,749	$—
2	$1,002,169	$531,580	$1,063,159	$1,601,711	$—
3	$1,013,093	$588,618	$1,177,236	$1,580,678	$—
4	$1,023,021	$557,657	$1,115,314	$1,667,530	$—
5	$1,033,251	$634,279	$1,268,558	$1,561,217	$—
6	$1,042,757	$518,460	$1,036,919	$1,654,233	$—
7	$1,052,872	$601,361	$1,202,723	$1,685,268	$—
8	$1,062,979	$622,289	$1,244,577	$1,727,928	$—
9	$1,073,716	$654,212	$1,308,424	$1,712,092	$—
10	$1,082,413	$629,679	$1,259,358	$1,737,101	$—
11	$1,093,129	$643,973	$1,287,946	$1,749,195	$—
12	$1,101,874	$647,321	$1,294,643	$1,804,491	$—
13	$1,112,892	$691,598	$1,383,197	$1,693,946	$—
14	$1,122,686	$571,260	$1,142,520	$1,733,416	$—
15	$1,135,821	$597,595	$1,195,191	$1,636,850	$—
16	$1,149,451	$487,399	$974,797	$1,675,120	$—
17	$1,161,060	$514,059	$1,028,119	$1,639,301	$36,298
18	$1,150,581	$488,719	$977,439	$1,778,394	$37,849
19	$1,141,972	$636,422	$1,272,843	$1,976,362	$40,052
20	$1,133,277	$843,084	$1,686,168	$2,048,768	$40,996
21	$1,125,404	$923,365	$1,846,730	$1,914,151	$39,821
22	$1,116,770	$797,381	$1,594,762	$1,963,433	$40,568
23	$1,106,263	$857,170	$1,714,340	$2,008,804	$41,260
24	$1,096,661	$912,143	$1,824,285	$2,151,119	$43,012

13. If the client is underfunded, then the cushion is zero. Without a cushion, there is no slack in the portfolio for taking risk. By analogy, the major Wall Street firms that have so recently become mere memories all suffered from too much leverage and the unwillingness to limit their risk taking by managing their excess equity (cushion) to protect their core equity (floor).

14. With an average return of over 13 percent on the risky portfolio, this client is indeed quite lucky. As the following table shows, with an ending portfolio value of $1.737 million, this client does not need to feel compelled to annuitize. Annuitization will offer the client the

opportunity to seek greater upside in retirement; that is, $1.737 million – $1.622 million provides less opportunity for future upside than $1.737 million – $1.424 million, but the decision becomes a matter of preference rather than necessity.

Age	Annuity Costs	Cushion	Risky Allocation	Ending Portfolio Value
50	$850,000	$150,000	$300,000	$998,670
51	$879,750	$118,920	$237,840	$1,000,472
52	$910,541	$89,931	$179,862	$1,049,925
53	$942,410	$107,515	$215,030	$1,022,305
54	$975,395	$46,911	$93,822	$1,060,718
55	$1,009,533	$51,185	$102,370	$1,108,314
56	$1,044,867	$63,447	$126,893	$1,163,777
57	$1,081,437	$82,339	$164,679	$1,210,815
58	$1,119,288	$91,528	$183,056	$1,249,475
59	$1,158,463	$91,012	$182,024	$1,330,946
60	$1,199,009	$131,938	$263,875	$1,389,415
61	$1,240,974	$148,441	$296,882	$1,431,751
62	$1,284,408	$147,342	$294,684	$1,463,185
63	$1,329,363	$133,822	$267,645	$1,566,854
64	$1,375,890	$190,964	$381,928	$1,622,787
65	$1,424,047	$198,741	$397,482	$1,737,403

15. If the rise in annuitization costs is random, then it becomes more prudent to manage the cushion to ensure that the floor at the next rebalancing is met (this is also true in the nonrandom case if there is a wide gap between rebalancing dates—a fact we conveniently ignored in Problem 14).

   In this case, the client isn't nearly as lucky, even though the overall return on the risky portfolio is a stellar 13 percent in the first four years, return on average is below −3.4 percent, which knocks the client into the annuity by age 54:

Age	Actual Annuity Costs	Potential Floor Cost	Cushion	Risky Allocation	Ending Portfolio Value
50	$850,000	$875,500	$124,500	$249,000	$950,276
51	$880,940	$907,368	$42,908	$85,816	$962,725
52	$924,370	$952,101	$10,624	$21,248	$985,458
53	$954,597	$983,235	$2,223	$4,446	$1,004,162
54	$988,008	$1,017,648	$—	$—	$—

The Transition Phase

1. The earliest practical date to begin transitioning the portfolio toward retirement income is when flooring for retirement can be acquired. Usually, this would be thought of as 30 years prior to the date of the first retirement cash flow.

2. Rollover distributions into an IRA are a way to effect the transition in a tax-efficient fashion. Individual advisers currently have a great advantage over sponsored plans, both in the ability to provide advice (assuming proper registration) and in the ability to customize portfolios for individual client needs. Using an IRA for the flooring portion of a retirement income portfolio allows the client to take full use of the tax deferral.

3. Using the tools that we created in the problems for Chapter 7, the answer is easy to determine. The natural transition point is right around the client's 41st birthday.

Age	Flooring Allocation
40	28.99%
41	29.84%
42	30.72%
43	31.62%
44	32.55%
45	33.51%

4. For a 45-year-old client, the allocation providing flooring at 4 percent of financial wealth is 33.51 percent. Since the client desires to keep the current allocation weights, transitioning the fixed income to flooring requires that we scale the allocation down to 30 percent. Since 33.51 percent implies a 4 percent floor, then the allocation percentage needs to be adjusted to 4% × 30% ÷ 33.51% = 3.581%. On a portfolio valued at $1,250,000, the annual flooring can be set at $44,763.

5. Using the table provided in Problem 3, we see the flooring allocation for this client is 28.99 percent. With a portfolio of $1,250,000, the client's allocation to flooring would be $362,356. If the IRA is used for flooring, then the remainder of the transition implies $112,356 to be allocated from the legacy portfolio. Since the funds in the IRA are fully allocated to flooring, the remainder of the flooring required will either be obtained over time via additional deposits or rollovers into the IRA or have to be located in the fully taxable account. If flooring is to be placed in the fully taxable account, then tax-exempt instruments may become advantageous. Ladders with whole bonds may be another possibility for creating flooring, using the current income to defray tax payments.

   If the client desired to hit the target allocations for retirement, then the advisor needs to understand whether the motivation for the moderately conservative portfolio was based on overall risk aversion or just an off-the-cuff attempt to ensure sufficient funds for protecting a retirement lifestyle.

6. The allocations don't necessarily need to change. It depends on the value of the portfolio relative to the cost of the floor and the multiplier. With active risk management, changing the focus of the portfolio doesn't, by necessity, mean changing the allocations. It does mean being ready to act if action is required.

   The main differentiator between the accumulation focus and retirement income focus requires that—except for cash and any ladder of bonds—an existing accumulation portfolio be thought of as equivalent to the upside component of a retirement income portfolio. Remember that bond funds of constant duration or indeterminate maturity do not count as flooring. They are at best a bet that when the funds are needed, rates won't be so high as to negatively affect lifestyle.

7. Naturally, some of the answer depends on whether you adhere to a "prudent man" or "prudent expert" standard. The answer also depends a bit on whether the client's self-directed choices are clearly recorded. However, the transition process is designed to prepare a client's portfolio for focusing more closely on retirement income through time. The transition is to get client's portfolios on and moving down the path of retirement income, over time. Many clients will end up with retirements that are underfunded.

   The action plan for this client can be to begin to set up a portfolio for floor plus upside, allowing the client to attempt to build the floor over time. If the client is successful, then the supposition about the client's prospects may have been unwarranted, but the actions did no harm. On the flipside, if the client is unsuccessful, there will have been a floor set up off of which the client can base the next decision on retirement timing, lifestyle, or annuitization. Except for the increased cost of annuitization due to surviving through what would have been a deferral period, the actions did no harm but kept the client's options open.

CHAPTER 11

Putting Together the Proposal

The problems for this chapter are qualitative in nature and require that you use your current tools. Therefore, no solutions are provided.

A few pointers from the text are worth repeating or elaborating from a slightly different vantage point:

1. *Start with the funds in the fixed-income portion of the accumulation portfolio.* A constant duration bond fund may have some desirable properties, but it does not constitute a secure floor. Let's consider a hypothetical client who will need the money in 15 years. If the funds are needed in 15 years, then the payment can be secured with a bond-type instrument or set of instruments that will mature on schedule. Ignoring the normal shape of the yield curve for a second, having a long-term bond fund as the lifestyle-securing instrument is equivalent to rolling a bet on long-term rates for 15 years. On the other hand, with a maturing instrument, the mark-to-market volatility will be declining as the instrument converges to its payoff amount. A corollary is that with the shape of the yield curve typically upward sloped it does imply some degradation in expected return.

2. *Remember the importance of tax location.* Creating a floor is important, but location of the floor in terms of taxability should not be overlooked. Placing a capital markets floor in a fully taxable account may create phantom income problems that the client will want to avoid. Here is a good time to raise the potential for taking a rollover distribution from a 401(k) and creating the flooring in an IRA. For many clients in the mass affluent categories, their 401(k)s/IRAs can comprise their flooring portfolios and their predominantly capital-gains-eligible upside can reside in fully taxable accounts.

   The big exception to the rule here are clients who are flooring with insurance products. Since insurance products already contain a tax deferral, then unless it is unavoidable, it is an inefficient waste of tax shields to place insurance products in a tax-deferred account.

3. *A comprehensive plan doesn't mean an immediate portfolio shift.* It is important to show the client where you are trying to take them, but it doesn't require a drastic change in composition. Ultimately, the client may need to secure and protect a floor. They may need various types of insurance for disability, care, and other individual-specific risks, but that doesn't mean that they need them today. There is some evidence from the marketing literature that as people age they become more resistant to both explicit and implicit hard-sell tactics. That means that it is doubly important to put together a proposal that keeps the client transition at a pace that is comfortable.

4. *Know which lifestyle category best describes the client.* The proposal should take into account the likely path or possible paths that the client will follow. Sometimes it is clear where the client will end up in terms of flooring type and retirement lifestyle. Haranguing a client about the need to save more is useless. However, by showing the path they are on, they might take concrete steps to alter their trajectory. Even if they stay on their current path, fewer surprises mean a more comfortable transition.

5. *Stress the flooring as the floor.* Life-cycle portfolios are designed to have asymmetric payoffs, floor plus upside. Do not neglect the importance of potential for upside. The flooring amount is the minimum consumption level that the client is willing to contemplate. One of your goals is to create a portfolio that makes the client comfortable that the floor will be exceeded by *some* amount. The lower that the consumption floor can be fixed relative to wealth, the more potential that there will be for upside in the portfolio. The objective is to minimize the floor without shortchanging it or diminishing its importance.

6. *Creating an asymmetric portfolio changes the client's view of risk.* The value of a call option increases as volatility increases. The asymmetric portfolio profiles that result from a floor plus upside configuration gives the client an incentive to want more risk in the upside portfolio. Even if the immediate changes are proposed only for the fixed-income portion of the portfolio, it may be worthwhile to gauge the client's tolerance toward risk in the remaining portion of the portfolio.

CHAPTER 12

Market Segmentation

1. When the consumption floor is zero, then the entire portfolio is constructed as the "upside" portfolio. To the client, the important issue would be for the upside to have the correct risk-return characteristics. In the risk-return tradeoff, since risk and return are linked, knowing the desired level of risk is sufficient for characterizing the proper portfolio type for the client. The segmentation along wealth dimensions is derived from the different wealth cohorts of investors having different desires for products and services.

2. In the presence of a consumption floor, clients differentiate themselves by their ability to fund their consumption. In the framework presented here, there are three segments: underfunded, constrained, and simple.

3. In a lifestyle segmentation, suitability risk can be somewhat reduced. By splitting the portfolio into floor and upside, the onus for suitability lies mainly on the quality of the floor. Secondarily is the traditional question of suitability in the upside portfolio. With the presence of a well-diversified or high-quality floor, the suitability concerns for the upside portfolio can be mitigated and vice versa.

4. Gross margins are high for mass-market and ultra-high net worth products for different reasons. The mass-market products tend to be simple products that are sold in price-competitive markets on small tickets having higher proportional transactions costs. At the ultra-high-net-worth end of the spectrum, the products tend to be more differentiated and less price competitive, although being more complex there are higher production costs.

5. If the client is characterized by habit formation, then their funding relative to wealth will be largely unchanged as wealth changes. As wealth rises, the needs of the habit former will rise. For someone immune to

habit formation, then a change in wealth will translate to a change in relative lifestyle.

6. Age determines allocation. However, with the exception of products that are designed specifically for people at the point of retirement, age doesn't really require separate product sets, just separate allocations.

CHAPTER 13

Products and Example Portfolios

There are no formal problems for this chapter, but there are some themes that drive the examples used in the text. What follows is an elaboration of the "art" behind the example and sample portfolios.

THE ENVIRONMENT

Most financial advisers operate in an environment that specializes in a client segment and product classification. While many capital markets advisers have insurance licenses and vice versa, most gravitate to a reusable playbook for capturing and serving clients. With a few glaring exceptions that we'll get to in a minute, the same themes of specialization and reusability can be carried into the creation of life-cycle or retirement portfolios.

As we've gone through the book, you've probably come to the realization that many of the changes to portfolio construction that are required lead to sales and advisory models centered on creating outcomes versus expectations. For the most part, the basic building-block products that are currently available are easily adapted to the difference in focus.

One underdeveloped part of the product space is in the area of bundling the building blocks. There are few capital market fund choices for providing flooring; fewer still for flooring plus upside. There are many fund choices for the symmetric portfolios of accumulation, but the fund industry has yet to fully exploit the idea of creating portfolios with asymmetric payoffs. A second area for development is in pure longevity insurance. While there have been some attempts at unbundling insurance products into components, they have mostly been enfeebled by extraordinarily high margins and inept marketing. But to paraphrase a former Secretary of Defense, we have to build portfolios with the tools we have, not the tools we want.

For the immediate and near term, that means that choices for flooring are limited. There are gaps in the product spectrum that we can't count on being filled soon. There are Treasury strips and then a large gap to bond ladders, followed by another gap to insurance-based annuities. Some hybrid solutions are available but they are not currently in wide distribution.

FOCUSING THE CLIENT

People like to acquire things, but there is also a strong desire to build and achieve milestones. The desire to achieve is something that can be harnessed to make for better outcomes for the client. A floor-plus-upside portfolio has two features that make it ideal for goal-seeking behavior: Outcomes are tangible and can be measurably influenced by behavior.

Saving more in the flooring subportfolio has a direct translation into payoff amounts. The result is both tangible and can be measurably influenced by behavior. While not arguing that there is an illusion of value, the discount nature of future notional values doesn't hurt. Even if inflation is misjudged and the flooring is not fully immunized, saving more today leads to a direct and compounded impact on future cash flows. For people exhibiting goal-seeking behavior, the attractiveness of creating flooring can alter behavior.

Saving more in the upside subportfolio has an impact nearly identical to the results for an accumulation portfolio with one major difference. Saving more in an upside subportfolio is equivalent to buying call options. With flooring in place, the downside is limited so as to not endanger lifestyle. In total and in tandem with the flooring subportfolio, with a balanced approach to flooring and upside, the weight of goal seeking can be borne by flooring and aspirations are levered on the upside portion.

Saving more in an accumulation portfolio means that expectation is higher, but the dollar variance is also higher. There is a better opportunity for success but there is no guarantee of even minimum performance. This means that the accumulation portfolio bears the weight of both aspirations and tangible goals. The client ends up with too much risk for their goals and insufficient risk for their aspirations.

FRAMING THE CLIENT

Would your client be best suited to an active or a passive portfolio approach? Is your client's lifestyle lavish relative to wealth, simple or somewhere in between? Clients choose the information that they are willing to reveal. From the information provided, the hope is to propose and implement a portfolio solution that leads to a contented client and more business.

Age is the one dimension on which clients usually reveal information—at least for the person with whom you deal directly. It is important to remember that the person you deal with is often not the entire client unit. A married client where the spouse is of a similar age has different needs from a client where the ages are significantly different. The person you deal with may only represent a fraction of the client unit. Many decisions that couples make are happily delegated during working careers; client income, expenses, and needs should refer to the unit not just the delegated representative.

The easiest bifurcation to make is between clients who prefer passive portfolios versus those who will prefer active risk management. There is an age dimension to this as the present value of any nominal flooring amount will be lower for a younger client. Other things equal, a younger client who is fully funded will have a portfolio with more of a cushion thus enabling higher exposure to risky assets. However, that statement implies a determination that the client is fully funded, to at least some defined floor amount.

Lifestyle relative to wealth and level of wealth are somewhat trickier. Generally, an adviser has verifiable information only on the fraction of financial wealth sitting in the account. In a purely transactional relationship, that is sufficient for the client to build their own retirement income portfolio. However, in a planning or asset-based capacity you want more information. You want information about wealth level to know their proper product cohort (see Chapter 12 in the main book). You want to know about their relative lifestyle to know the appropriate class of flooring solution.

In the main book, we have differentiated client lifestyles into three types. The simple lifestyle has the greatest capacity, though perhaps the least interest, for active management. The simple lifestyle also has the most options available for choosing among the classes of flooring solutions: capital markets, hybrid, and insurance. At the underfunded end of the spectrum, clients are more likely to need to monetize their mortality regardless of their preferences and even that may not be sufficient for them to meet their lifestyle needs. Underfunded clients are the most likely to need to reevaluate their plans and preferences and least likely to be satisfied.

SUMMARIZING THE PROCESS

- Active passive typing
  - Preferences for taking risk
  - Preferences toward portfolio activity

- Age helps determine
  - Accumulation potential
  - Options open to the client
- Relative lifestyle
  - Feasibility of flooring solutions
  - Capacity for managed approaches
  - Necessity of adjusting client expectations
- Wealth
  - Appropriate product types
- Other personal characteristics
  - Necessitate nonstandard solutions

CHAPTER 14

Preparing Your Client
for a Retirement Income Portfolio

There are no formal problems for this chapter, but as you go through some of the processes illustrated by the checklist for ownership of responsibility provided for this chapter in Part One of the workbook, you may want to think about the following issues.

BIG PICTURE

Let your clients know the big picture first. If they understand where you are going with your questions and where you are trying to take them with their portfolio, they will be more open with information.

Balance Sheet

Assets Clients, particularly new clients, often begin by keeping information close to the vest. Trust can be gained and the relationship deepened over time. You don't need to gain full information at the start of the process.

Financial Capital Clients expect a line of questioning on financial assets and are prepared to divulge most of their financial assets. Having the client maintain a small "betting" portfolio at a discount house is okay and is preferable to fielding calls every day inquiring about a small punt that he or she has taken. The OTB (off-track betting) model of investment promulgated by the business networks needs to grab the viewer's attention and may be counterproductive in building or maintaining wealth. But such programming has an impact. Parents often warn their kids that too much TV can make them stupid. The business networks pull off the rare two-for-one by also leaving devotees poorer.

The real assets owned by the client are often put under the heading of financial capital. Regardless of where you place real assets, remember that completeness is more useful than the compartment in which the assets are placed. Asking about homes, both primary and secondary residences are natural questions, but avoid accepting high-water mark values. Cars, boats, and other assets with substantial monetary value may be lurking or gathering dust. Over the years, many people accumulate things of great value that are often overlooked. Asking about hobbies or inherited artwork, stamps or coins can sometimes unmask amounts of wealth about which the client is unaware. Questions of this sort often uncover more than just wealth; they can uncover a common interest and lead to new prospects.

One of the sensitivities with real assets is that people generally like them. That is, assets are typically held for their inherent value in creating a happier life. They provide utility. Therefore, clients may be unwilling to part with them. Rather than leaving them off the table, my preference is to list them as assets but fudge by creating a contra-asset underneath, which has the effect of writing down the asset value. That way the asset is listed as a potential source of funds if unforeseen events create a scramble for funds.

Human Capital   Clients usually tell you what they do before they tell you what they make. To get this important bit of data, you need to be clear about how the information will be used. The goal is twofold: understand their lifestyle relative to their cash flow and then determine the asset value of their earning power. For discounting their human capital, a beta adjustment reflecting the risk of their industry is usually worthwhile. Make sure to ask about pensions for which they may be eligible.

Social Capital   Most of your clients are probably eligible for Social Security income (SSI). The SSI sum may seem small, but it is an important and inflation-protected part of the floor for most clients. Veterans, particularly those who sustained combat injuries that may become debilitating in the future, may be entitled to benefits. There may be other claims on cash flows to which the client is entitled that fall outside the bounds of what are considered human capital and financial capital.

Liabilities   Liabilities are tricky to measure. There are current commitments and future commitments that must be met. Then there is the spectrum that begins at needs, covers wants, and ends at fantasies. The important image to keep in mind is that your role here entails listening while whittling. You'll want to whittle the initial needs list down to leave only the true core needs. You shouldn't apply a moral judgment to decide what a legitimate lifestyle need for the client is; but you have to listen to distinguish the important from the unimportant.

Mortgages and Loans   Most of your clients have mortgages and other forms of debt. Most of the debt comes with a payoff amount or remaining balance. This type of information tends to be readily available and easy to incorporate in the client balance sheet.

Preretirement Consumption Needs   The preretirement needs are an important component of the client balance sheet and can act as an important control instrument. Remember though, needs are discounted at the risk-free rate: needs *must* be met.

You want to separate current spending levels into those which cover the lifestyle needs of the client and those which are harder to explain. Many clients spend thousands of dollars per year on purchases that are related to wants and whims rather than core expenditures. Since amounts on the balance sheet are easily shifted from one category to another, a powerfully visceral linkage can be made between current expenditures that are unimportant and future needs that need to be met.

Full confession: At one point I had a wine cellar that was on the verge of becoming larger than any amount of wine that I would ever enjoy. Expenditures were always well within my budget but, in retrospect, not remotely necessary to my lifestyle. More useful than mere budgeting, the balance sheet illustrates opportunity cost. While what is there is aging nicely and gathering dense layers of dust, the explicitly calculated prospect of a higher retirement floor has enticed me away from adding to my wine cellar.

Postretirement Consumption Needs   The same tendency to confuse wants for needs that acts as a drag on the rate of saving during the earning years permeates initial thoughts about postretirement. Many clients have not thought about the run rate of their lifestyle costs nor do they realize how long they are likely to survive. Going through this with clients is time consuming. Time is precious, so you'll want them to take a good stab at this on their own. The task at hand is to help the client define their needs and list their wants.

The goal isn't to minimize the floor but to find the right floor. Few clients are in a position where their assets are ample for full realization of their retirement desires with unlimited longevity; they have limits. But knowing limits doesn't mean ending up miserable. Whether the limits are known or unknown, misery follows from exceeding limits.

There may be some needs that fall outside of the standard needs that one would normally envision. Food and shelter are needs that must be met as flows year after year. But there may be other expenses that are also viewed as needs entailing one-time outlays. As examples, a client may intend to move toward an assisted-living facility, have promised to pay for a wedding, educate a child, or even to bury themselves in a certain style.

Discretionary Wealth   In the client balance sheet, discretionary wealth can be initially thought of as a plug to keep the balance in the balance sheet. The amount of discretionary wealth on the balance sheet can be found by subtracting total liabilities from total assets. But this same concept of discretionary wealth serves the dual purpose of providing the opportunity to achieve the financial aspirations of the client. Discretionary wealth is the basis for the upside portfolio, and it is also a source of funding for the client's wants.

For the upside portfolio, the degree of a client's risk aversion will impact both the composition of the upside portfolio and the rate for drawing down discretionary wealth. Clients who are more risk averse, or whose risk aversion increases as wealth is drawn down, will want a less risky upside portfolio and will want to draw down the upside portfolio at a slower initial rate. Clients who are more tolerant of risk will be willing to both take more risk in their upside portfolios and draw down the upside portfolio at a faster initial rate.

Pro Forma Income and Cash Flow Statements

For a plan or client proposal to be considered comprehensive the clients will want to know what they can expect each year in income. Lay out the sources and uses of cash flows. As a matter of form, breaking up the income into the pieces coming from flooring sources and the part coming from discretionary wealth subportfolios makes for a more credible experience. One thing that should be illuminated is to show whether the flooring extends into extreme old age. For my purposes, I like to see it extend out to age 105 since the century club isn't as exclusive as it used to be.

Risks and Uncertainties

Client lifestyles are threatened by myriad risks and uncertainties. The risks are usually well-defined events that occur with enough regularity to estimate probabilities and outcomes. Uncertainties tend to be more diffuse and abstract events that are too rare for quantification. Both can cause harm to the client. Even those outcomes that you are unable to provide direct assistance in avoiding can be discussed.

If your primary business orientation is insurance products, then you are in a good position to ameliorate many of the individual risks that retirees face. Both the physical and financial impacts of health-related risks are a major source of fear for retirees. Ironically, it is the healthiest at the point of retirement who are most likely to benefit from coverage such as long-term care insurance; they are likely to live long enough to need care.

If your primary business orientation is capital markets products, then you are in a good position to ameliorate most of the market and credit risks that retirees face. Both the market risk and particularly the credit risk of flooring in portfolios need to be carefully considered for clients whose portfolio will be depleted during retirement. With no backup capability to start over, one of the last things that you want is for your client to have a concentrated position that has the potential to destroy their lifestyle.

Uncertainties are harder to protect against, particularly since many that can impact the client are unknowable. However, uncertain events—everything from frequent but unknowable events like tax policy change to the rare devastating natural disaster—can usually be categorized by the impact that they can have on the individual constituents of the balance sheet, income statement, or cash flow statement.

CHAPTER 15

Salvage Operations, Mistakes, and Fallacies

1. If the shares of ABC are shorted, and the proceeds placed into a risk-free account then the account will draw interest of 2.5 percent (risk-free rate less borrow costs), but the short seller also needs to make the dividend payments to the actual owner of the borrowed shares. Therefore the quarterly growth on the account holding the proceeds of the short sale will be .00625 = (1/4) × 2.5% less $0.60. For clarity of exposition, I include the first three quarters of accrual in the table of results.

Period	Proceeds in Short Account
Q1	$10,027.50
Q2	$10,055.24
Q3	$10,083.22
1 Year	$10,111.45
3 Years	$10,346.35
5 Years	$10,598.21
10 Years	$11,310.28
25 Years	$14,367.83

One can see quite readily that the proceeds of the short sale grow slowly, more slowly than the risk-free rate.

2. Neither the expected return nor the volatility, in fact none of the parameters of the probability distribution underlying ABC matter for the proceeds of the short position.

3. The counterparty who agrees to buy ABC 15 years from today does not want to take uncompensated risk; therefore the counterparty will offer a price commensurate with maintaining a hedged position: The counterparty will short ABC today and place the proceeds in a risk-free account. Paying the costs of borrowing shares and the dividends will

lower the rate below risk free. In this example, the most that the counterparty will offer your client is $121.58. In all likelihood, the offered price will be somewhat lower due to uncertainty about future borrow costs (borrow costs are short-term rates that can change) and future dividends.

Moral of the story: No matter how great the stock or portfolio looks on paper, there's no way to lock in hope.

4. For the risk-free portfolio, the value can be found by calculating $V_T = V_0 e^{r_f T}$. For this problem, that works out to $\$1,000,000 e^{10 \times .03} = \$1,349,859$.

5. For the risky portfolio, the value can be found by calculating $V_T = V_0 e^{rT}$. For this problem that works out to $\$1,000,000 e^{10 \times .08} = \$2,225,541$.

6. After 10 years, the $1,000,000 initial portfolio, assuming a lognormal distribution with a Z value of -1.645 implies that the portfolio will be worth:

$$V_T = \$1,000,000 e^{\left(.08 - \frac{.15^2}{2}\right)10 - 0.15 \times 1.645\sqrt{10}} = \$911,383$$

7. Setting the Z values equal:

$$V_T = \$1,000,000 e^{\left(.08 - \frac{.15^2}{2}\right)10 + 0.15 \times Z\sqrt{10}} = \$1,000,000 e^{.03 \times 10}$$

$$\Rightarrow \left(.08 - \frac{.15^2}{2}\right)10 + 0.15 \times Z\sqrt{10} = .30$$

$$\Rightarrow Z = \frac{.30 - \left(.08 - \frac{.15^2}{2}\right)10}{.15\sqrt{10}} \approx -.817$$

This means that even under the well-behaved lognormal distribution, the portfolio has more than a 20 percent probability of underperforming the risk-free rate after 10 years.

8. For general portfolios of arbitrary risk-free return, expected risky return, variance and length of time, the portfolios are of equal value when the following is true:

$$V_T = V_0 e^{\left(r - \frac{\sigma^2}{2}\right)T + \sigma \times Z\sqrt{T}} = V_0 e^{r_f T}$$

$$\Rightarrow \left(r - \frac{\sigma^2}{2}\right)T + \sigma \times Z\sqrt{T} = r_f T$$

$$\Rightarrow Z = -\frac{\left(r - r_f - \frac{\sigma^2}{2}\right)T}{\sigma\sqrt{T}} = -\left(\frac{r - r_f}{\sigma}\right)\sqrt{T} + \frac{1}{2}\sigma\sqrt{T}$$

Not surprisingly (after the fact) this result is a direct analog to the Sharpe ratio. Notice how the two parts act as countervailing forces, with the left-hand term providing the optimism and the right-hand term the cause for concern.

This can be taken one step further if we take a CAPM view and write the expected return on the portfolio p as $r_p = \alpha_p + \beta_p \text{MRP}$, where MRP represents the market risk premium $r_{\text{market}} - r_f$ allowing for the possibility of α, for purposes of illustration, and the standard deviation as $\sigma_p = \sqrt{\beta_p^2 \sigma_m^2 + \sigma_{p_i}^2}$, where the second term inside the square root operator denotes any nonsystematic risk that remains. We return to the Sharpe ratio expression above to substitute in

$$Z = -\left(\frac{r - r_f}{\sigma}\right)\sqrt{T} + \frac{1}{2}\sigma\sqrt{T}$$

$$= -\left(\frac{\alpha_p + \beta_p \text{MRP}}{\sqrt{\beta_p^2 \sigma_m^2 + \sigma_{p_i}^2}}\right)\sqrt{T} + \frac{1}{2}\sqrt{\beta_p^2 \sigma_m^2 + \sigma_{p_i}^2}\,\sqrt{T}$$

Examining the preceding shows that if the portfolio we use is not well diversified then a hurdle is raised and the probability of underperforming the risk-free asset increases for any time T.

If we restrict ourselves to well-diversified portfolios, then the expression simplifies a bit to the following:

$$Z = -\left(\frac{r - r_f}{\sigma}\right)\sqrt{T} + \frac{1}{2}\sigma\sqrt{T}$$

$$= -\left(\frac{\alpha_p + \beta_p \text{MRP}}{\sqrt{\beta_p^2 \sigma_m^2}}\right)\sqrt{T} + \frac{1}{2}\sqrt{\beta_p^2 \sigma_m^2}\,\sqrt{T}$$

$$= -\left(\frac{\alpha_p + \beta_p \text{MRP}}{|\beta_p|\sigma_m}\right)\sqrt{T} + \frac{1}{2}|\beta_p|\sigma_m\sqrt{T}$$

Finally, if we do not want to assume that free money (excess return without risk), α, exists and restrict to portfolios with $\beta > 0$, then we get the further simplification:

$$Z = -\left(\frac{r - r_f}{\sigma}\right)\sqrt{T} + \frac{1}{2}\sigma\sqrt{T}$$

$$- \left(\frac{\text{MRP}}{\sigma_m}\right)\sqrt{T} + \frac{1}{2}|\beta_p|\sigma_m\sqrt{T}$$

This means that the *assumption* of a future market risk premium provides a source of optimism, but that the higher the degree of market risk taken in a portfolio the greater the chance of underperforming the risk-free asset at any time interval.

9. This client is in pretty good shape for retirement income. Two paths to consider would be a passive approach to create flooring for the client using 90 percent of the current portfolio with the rest being split somehow between longevity, precautionary, and risky. The less viable path to take would be to take more risk and try to actively risk manage the account. However, since there is only a 10 percent cushion (excluding precautionary and longevity needs) there is little room for error and, depending on dollar value, there may not be sufficient assets to warrant active risk management.

10. The Z value for missing the target requirement for retirement would be where

$$\$1,000,000e^{.03} = \$1,000,000e^{\left(\left(.1-\frac{.14^2}{2}\right)+.14Z\right)}$$

$$\Rightarrow .03 = \left(.1 - \frac{.14^2}{2}\right) + .14Z$$

$$\Rightarrow Z = -.43$$

This result implies a 33 percent probability of failure using the normal distribution.

11. All told, the Everetts are not in bad shape. Their lifestyle needs are still fully funded, although their upside has been curtailed. The Everetts can be served by choosing to either take the path of an active risk management or a passive approach with more risk in their upside portfolio.

12. The client aged 34 would consume

$$f_t^{Pct} = \frac{1}{T-t+1} = \frac{1}{105-34+1} = \frac{1}{72} \approx 1.4\%$$

of wealth this year.

The client aged 56 would consume

$$f_t^{Pct} = \frac{1}{T-t+1} = \frac{1}{105-56+1} = \frac{1}{50} = 2.0\%$$

of wealth this year.

The client aged 66 would consume

$$f_t^{Pct} = \frac{1}{T-t+1} = \frac{1}{105-66+1} = \frac{1}{40} = 2.5\%$$

of wealth this year.

13. This client's economic balance sheet and consumption are given by the following:

Assets		Liabilities	
Human capital		Mortgage	$800,000
PV earnings @4%	$1,758,849		
Financial capital			
Portfolio	$250,000		
House	$1,000,000	Net wealth	$2,208,849
Total	$3,008,849		$3,008,849

This hypothetical client would spend right around 1.4 percent of $2,158,848 = $30,678.46 this year. (The amount seems low because we are using a very simple construct and we put in a very long retirement for this client to fund.)

14. If the client suffers a 40 percent decline in portfolio value, the new balance sheet will be the following:

Assets		Liabilities	
Human capital		Mortgage	$800,000
PV earnings	$1,758,849		
Financial capital			
Portfolio	$150,000		
House	$1,000,000	Net wealth	$2,108,849
Total	$2,908,849		$2,908,849

The new consumption will be $29,289.57. Net a 40 percent decline in portfolio value led to a 5 percent decline in economic wealth and a 5 percent decline in consumption.

15. Our client gets laid off for a full year, but retains expectations that are for a full recovery afterward; the new balance sheet will be the following:

Assets		Liabilities	
Human capital		Mortgage	$800,000
PV earnings	$1,662,696		
Financial capital			
Portfolio	$250,000		
House	$1,000,000	Net wealth	$2,112,696
Total	$2,912,696		$2,912,696

The new level of consumption will be $29,342.99. Net a full year layoff led to a 4 percent decline in economic wealth and a 4 percent decline in consumption.

16. Fear and uncertainty about maintaining future employment (or employment earnings) lead to implicitly higher discount rates applied to future earnings. In this example, we discount future earnings at 5 percent.

Assets		Liabilities	
Human capital		Mortgage	$800,000
PV earnings	$1,559,281		
Financial capital			
Portfolio	$250,000		
House	$1,000,000	Net wealth	$2,009,281
Total	$2,809,281		$2,809,281

The new level of consumption will be $27,906.68. Even without getting laid off, fear about the future led to a 9 percent decline in economic wealth and a 9 percent decline in consumption.

17. If housing prices fall by 40 percent the new balance sheet will be given by the following:

Assets		Liabilities	
Human capital		Mortgage	$800,000
PV earnings	$1,758,849		
Financial capital			
Portfolio	$250,000		
House	$600,000	Net wealth	$1,808,849
Total	$2,608,849		$2,608,849

Consumption will be $25,122.91 which is an 18 percent drop.

18. In our simple example the largest drops were from drops in housing prices and increased uncertainty about future income. The smallest drops were from declines in financial portfolios and temporary layoffs.

These simple examples illustrate that assets, like housing, taking up a large fraction of personal balance sheets can have an outsized impact on consumption (pro or con). The other large contributor was the higher discount rate on future earnings. The collapse in consumption that occurred among wage earners last fall was tied more closely to peak levels of uncertainty, that is, raising the discount rate on future earnings rather than the interrelated problems of actual layoffs, the two-year trend of declines in housing prices, or the movement of securities prices.

Printed and bound by CPI Group (UK) Ltd, Croydon, CR0 4YY

16/04/2025

14658524-0001